Manitoba at Christmas

Manitoba at Christmas
HOLIDAY MEMORIES IN THE KEYSTONE PROVINCE

Edited by Wayne Chan

MANITOBA AT CHRISTMAS: HOLIDAY MEMORIES IN THE KEYSTONE PROVINCE

Copyright © 2016 by Wayne Chan

All rights reserved. No part of this book may be reproduced or transmitted in any form or by any means, electronic or mechanical, including photocopying, recording or by any information storage and retrieval system, without written permission of the publisher.

ISBN–13: 978-0-9921622-1-4 (softcover)

1. Christmas—Manitoba. 2. Manitoba—Social life and customs. I. Chan, Wayne.

Printed by IngramSpark
1st Printing: November, 2016

Cover design: Caitlin Blackmore

To my parents

Christmas in Manitoba

An English Christmas is apt to show
Very diversified kinds of weather;
Sometimes sunshine, rarely snow,
oftener slush and drizzle together,
And lovers of skating are apt to pronounce
Old Father Christmas a bit of a bounce!

In Manitoba it is not so,
Christmas is sure to be nipping and cold;
And as our sledge glides over the snow,
We do not ask if the frost will hold;
We are more in the habit of searching for traces
Of frost-bite, lest noses should drop off from faces.

—*The Graphic*, Christmas Number, 1878

Contents

Contents	1
Introduction	5
Christmas Stories: Holiday Memories in Manitoba	7
Jens Eriksen Munk — Christmas in Nova Dania	9
Samuel Hearne — Hearne's Third Expedition	11
Robert M. Ballantyne — To Absent Friends	13
Alexandre-Antonin Taché — Archbishop Taché's First Christmas in Manitoba	17
Joseph J. Hargrave — A Red River Christmas	21
John J. Gunn — The Festive Season in the Olden Days	25
Anonymous — Christmas Morning on the Red River Settlement	27
An Old Resident — How Riel's Prisoners Got Their Christmas Dinners	29
Anonymous — A Notable Dinner at Fort Garry	31
Mary FitzGibbon — A Christmas Ball	35
George Simpson McTavish — Christmas at York Factory	37
Emma Louisa Averill — Christmas at the Averill Homestead	41
Nellie McClung — Spruce Boughs and Apple-Jelly Tarts	45
Salome Halldorson — Icelandic Christmas	47
Winnipeg Daily Tribune — One of the Finest Christmas Displays Ever Seen	49
Gladys McKay — Santa Claus is a Good Lad	53
William A. Czumer — The First Galician Christmas at Bachman School	55
Ruth Walker Harvey — A World of Wonders	59
Verena Garrioch — Turning Back Memory's Happiest Pages	67
Arthur R. Devlin — Christmas at Asessippi	71
Charles Douglas Richardson — Thinking of Home	73
Evelina Adams — The Spanish Flu Comes to Neepawa	77
Mabel E. Finch — Christmas in a New Canadian School	79
Winnipeg Evening Tribune — Santa and His Marvels Come Back to City	83
Winnipeg Evening Tribune — Little Girl's Wish Brings Santa to Hudson's Bay	87

Vera Fryer ~ Next Stop, Pine Falls 89
Rose Fyleman ~ Winnipeg at Christmas 90
Wayne Chan ~ How "Winnipeg at Christmas" Came to Pass 91
Joseph Payjack, Jr. ~ Riding the Rods 93
Eileen Wilson ~ A Vignette of a Winnipeg Winter 95
Margaret Laurence ~ Upon a Midnight Clear 97
Alice and David Didur ~ Ukrainian Christmas on the Homestead 103
Marcel Pitre ~ Happenings From Our Farm 105
King George VI ~ The King's Speech, Christmas 1939 107
Margaret Dennis Owen ~ The Home Front 111
Evelyn Ballantyne ~ Christmas Wish 115
Gordon Billings ~ Christmas at Our House 117
Mary Louise Chown ~ Who Are The Saints? 121
Wayne Chan ~ Going to the Big City: Shopping at Eaton's 123
Judy Gerstel ~ A Tale of Christmas Past at Eaton's 129
Grace Warkentin ~ Memories of the Last Day Before Christmas 131
Winnipeg Tribune ~ The Unknown Santa: Silver Dollar Is His Trademark . . . 135
Margaret V. Fast ~ The Spirit of Christmas 139
Petrosha ~ Oh Christmas Tree! 141
Trish Suzanne ~ Finnish Christmas Traditions 143
Donna Firby Gamache ~ A Christmas to Remember 145
Roger Currie ~ Guess Who's Coming to Dinner? 147
Theresa Oswald ~ My Best Present? My Brother 151
Leah Boulet ~ A Charlie Brown Tree 153
Wayne Chan ~ The Christmas Wreath 155
Erin Hammond ~ North of the Highway 157
Brandy Reid ~ Memories of Christmases Past 161
Martha Hochheim ~ Christmas at the Hochheims' 165
Jennifer Collerone ~ Crossing the Chief Peguis 167
Sheila McKay ~ On the Doorstep 169

Eat and Be Merry: Holiday Recipes in Manitoba   171
Eaton's Dark Fruitcake 173
CNR Plum Pudding 175
Vinarterta 176
Plumi Moos 178
Ukrainian Christmas Eve Holubtsi (Cabbage Rolls) 179
Pfeffernüsse 181
Slovak Kapustnica and Bobalky 183
Broccoli Casserole 186
Grandma's Shortbread 187

Christmas Sweets: Delectable Gifts That the Kitchen May Provide 188
Nan and Auntie Brenda's Guyanese Fruitcake 190
Stir-Me-Nots 192
Filipino-Style Grilled Pork Skewers 193
Alexander Küchen 194
Stuffing 195
Oatcakes 196
Tourtière 197
Finnish Cranberry Pudding 198
Slush Punch 199
Schuten Krapflen 200

Story Contributors   201

Recipe Contributors   210

Acknowledgements   213

Sources   215

Index   225

Robert Pelly, Governor of Red River, driving his family on the river in a horse carriole, ca. 1823–24.

Introduction

THERE IS A SCENE in Charles Dickens's *A Christmas Carol* where Scrooge and the Spirit of Christmas Present fly over the rooftops of England to observe the holiday celebrations at various locales—a market, Bob Cratchit's home, a miner's cottage, a lighthouse, a ship at sea, and finally, the home of Scrooge's nephew. This was Scrooge's second ghostly visitation of the night, having earlier been shown scenes of his childhood by the Spirit of Christmas Past.

I wish to take the reader on a similar Yuletide journey through time and space for our province of Manitoba—to show Christmas celebrations in different communities and at different times, much as the Spirits of Christmas Past and Present did in Dickens's tale. In our stories, the specific place may change and the era may change, but two common threads remain: the time of year and the province in which the stories take place.

We start with the earliest Christmases recorded in what is now Manitoba, written by explorers in search of a passage to the Far East. We then have accounts from lonely fur-trading outposts, where the holiday observances were often simple in nature—a glass raised in honour of the occasion and a remembrance of loved ones back home.

We move on to the establishment of the Red River Colony which ushered in the settler era. We will read of courageous pioneer families like the Averills, trying to survive the harsh winters of Manitoba while making the most of the holiday season. Then came the dawn of the 20th century, the Great War, the Spanish Flu pandemic, the Depression, and then World War II. Manitobans were on tenterhooks waiting to hear news of their loved ones after the fall of Hong Kong on Christmas Day in 1941, yet they tried to observe Christmas as best as they could under the circumstances.

As the calendar pages fall away, we make a trip to Eaton's in its hey-day, with its doormen and white-gloved elevator operators, and join our younger selves as we dash upstairs to see Santa's Toyland. Advancing through the latter half of the 20th century, we visit a succession of communities, from Steinbach to Bakers Narrows, and remember special times there.

Many of the stories have been written specifically for this anthology, while others have been reprinted from previously published works. Stories from early time periods have been researched and gathered from historical sources. Stories were included if they took place within the modern geographical boundaries of Manitoba, regardless of when the tale took place. I have tried to collect stories from all parts of the province and from diverse cultural groups, as well as a wide range of time periods. In some instances I have sought out stories from specific regions or peoples to fill a perceived gap in the anthology. If a particular group or a region was not represented, it is simply due to my being unable to find an appropriate story.

The contributors to the anthology came from all walks of life. Although some are professional writers, others are people who had heard of my project and wished to share a special Christmas memory, even if they hadn't picked up pen and paper since their school days.

The title of the anthology takes its inspiration from the iconic poem, *Winnipeg at Christmas* by Rose Fyleman, which is reprinted in this volume, along with the story of how the poem came about.

Some stories have been edited or abridged, but I have preferred to keep the changes to a minimum, to allow the author's voice to show through. In some of the early historical accounts, the language may occasionally sound a little pejorative to modern ears, but I have left these references unaltered as a reflection of the time period.

In addition to the holiday memories, the book also contains is a collection of holiday recipes mostly contributed by Manitobans. Similar to the stories, I have tried to gather recipes from different groups to represent the diversity of our province's population.

Christmas has always been a time for memories, and many of us have a Christmas that was particularly memorable, whether it was for happy or sad reasons. The stories in the anthology are a reflection of this. Some are heartwarming, some amusing, some sad or poignant. But they are all Yuletide stories by Manitobans, to be shared with all Manitobans. I hope that you enjoy reading them as much as I did.

Have a Merry Christmas!

Wayne Chan
Winnipeg

Christmas Stories: Holiday Memories in Manitoba

Christmas in Nova Dania

Jens Eriksen Munk
"Winterhaven" (approximately 6 km southwest of present-day Churchill), 1619

In May 1619, Dano-Norwegian explorer Jens Munk embarked on an ill-fated expedition in search of the Northwest Passage. By September, Munk's two ships, the Enhiörningen *(the Unicorn) and the* Lamprenen *(the Lamprey), had reached the western shore of Hudson Bay, which Munk claimed in the name of the King of Denmark, calling it, "Nova Dania" (New Denmark). Realizing that it was too late in the year to return to Europe, they were forced to overwinter in the Churchill River estuary, at a location Munk named* Vindterhaffn *("Winterhaven" or "Winter Harbour"). In* Navigatio Septentrionalis, *Munk's published diary of the expedition, he recounts that his men were still in good spirits at Christmas. This is one of the earliest recorded observances of Christmas in what is now Manitoba.*

ON THE 20TH OF December, the weather was fine and mild, so that the whole crew was on shore. A part of them went shooting, so that we might have some fresh meat for the approaching Christmas Holy Days; another part occupied themselves with getting wood and burning charcoal. In the evening, the men who had been out shooting returned and brought a number of ptarmigan and a hare.

On the 22nd of December, we had a sharp frost. I had a Rostock barrel filled with water; and, in the morning, when they loosened the hoops of the barrel, it was frozen quite to the bottom and was all ice.

On the 24th of December, which was Christmas Eve, I gave the men wine and strong beer, which they had to boil afresh, for it was frozen to the bottom; so they had quite as much as they could stand, and were very jolly, but no one offended another with as much as a word.

The Holy Christmas Day we all celebrated and observed solemnly, as a Christian's duty is. We had a sermon and Mass; and, after the sermon, we gave the priest an offertory, according to ancient custom, each in proportion to his means. There was not much money among the men, but they gave what they had; some of them gave white fox-skins, so that the priest got enough wherewith to line a coat. However, sufficiently long life to wear it was not granted to him.

During all the Holy Days, the weather was rather mild; and, in order that the time might not hang on hand, the men practised all kinds of games; and whoever could imagine the most amusement was the most popular. The crew, most of whom were, at that time, in good health, consequently had all sorts of larks and pastimes; and thus we spent the Holy Days with the merriment that was got up.

Continued on next page →

Woodcut of Munk's Winterhaven (Churchill River Estuary).

The high morale of Munk's crew was short-lived. They were ill-equipped for the long, severe winter that lay ahead and their living conditions began to rapidly deteriorate in the New Year. The 65 men of the expedition were decimated by scurvy and privation, and by June 1620 only Munk and two of his men were still alive. Miraculously, the three survivors were able to regain their strength in the spring, and on July 16, they began their voyage home in the **Lamprenen***, the smaller of the two ships, which normally required a crew of 16. They sighted Norway on September 20 and made landfall the next day. In Munk's words, "we poor men could not hold our tears for great joy, and thanked God that He had graciously granted us this happiness."*

Hearne's Third Expedition

Samuel Hearne
Egg River, 1770

The search for the Northwest Passage continued in the decades after Munk's expedition. Over 150 years later, Samuel Hearne set out on his third attempt to find an overland route. His first two expeditions ended in failure, but the third one ultimately proved successful. His party, led by Chipewyan guide Matonabbee, left York Factory on December 7, 1770. After arriving at the Egg River and discovering that their previously cached food supply had been pilfered, they observed Christmas on empty stomachs, with Hearne dreaming of Christmas dinner back home.

ON THE SEVENTH OF December I set out on my third journey; and the weather, considering the season of the year, was for some days pretty mild. One of Matonabbee's wives being ill, occasioned us to walk so slow, that it was the thirteenth before we arrived at Seal River; at which time two men and their wives left us, whose loads, when added to those of the remainder of my crew, made a very material difference, especially as Matonabbee's wife was so ill as to be obliged to be hauled on a sledge.

Finding deer and all other game very scarce, and not knowing how long it might be before we could reach any place where they were in greater plenty, the Indians walked as far each day as their loads and other circumstances would conveniently permit. On the sixteenth, we arrived at Egg River, where Matonabbee and the rest of my crew had laid up some provisions and other necessaries, when on their journey to the Fort. On going to the place where they thought the provisions had been carefully secured from all kinds of wild beasts, they had the mortification to find that some of their countrymen, with whom the Governor had first traded and dispatched from the Fort, had robbed the store of every article, as well as of some of their most useful implements. This loss was more severely felt, as there was a total want of every kind of game; and the Indians, not expecting to meet with so great a disappointment, had not used that economy in the expenditure of the oatmeal and other provisions which they had received at the Fort, as they probably would have done, had they not relied firmly on finding a supply at this place. This disappointment and loss was borne by the Indians with the greatest fortitude; and I did not hear one of them breathe the least hint of revenge in case they should ever discover the offenders; the only effect it had on them was that of making them put the best foot foremost. This was thought so necessary, that for some time we walked every day from morning till night. The days, however, being short, our sledges heavy, and some of the road very bad, our progress seldom exceeded sixteen or eighteen miles a day, and some days we did not travel so much.

On the eighteenth, as we were continuing our course to the North West, up a small creek that empties itself into Egg River, we saw the tracks of many deer which had crossed that part a few days before; at that time there was not a fresh track to be seen: some of the Indians, however, who had lately passed that way, had killed more than they had occasion for, so that several joints of good meat were found in their old tent-places; which, though only sufficient for one good meal, were very acceptable, as we had been in exceeding straitened circumstances for many days.

On the nineteenth, we pursued our course in the North West quarter; and, after leaving the above-mentioned creek, traversed nothing but entire barren ground, with empty bellies, till the twenty-seventh; for though we arrived at some woods on the twenty-sixth, and saw a few deer, four of which the Indians killed, they were at so great a distance from the place on which we lay, that it was the twenty-seventh before the meat was brought to the tents. Here the Indians proposed to continue one day, under pretence of repairing their sledges and snow shoes; but from the little attention they paid to those repairs, I was led to think that the want of food was the chief thing that detained them, as they never ceased eating the whole day. Indeed for many days before we had in great want, and for the last three days had not tasted a morsel of any thing, except a pipe of tobacco and a drink of snow water; and as we walked daily from morning till night, and were all heavy laden, our strength began to fail. I must confess that I never spent so dull a Christmas; and when I recollected the merry season which was then passing, and reflected on the immense quantities, and great variety of delicacies which were then expending in every part of Christendom, and that with a profusion bordering on waste, I could not refrain from wishing myself again in Europe, if it had been only to have had an opportunity of alleviating the extreme hunger which I suffered with the refuse of the table of any one of my acquaintance. My Indians, however, still kept in good spirits; and as we were then across all the barren ground, and saw a few fresh tracks of deer, they began to think that the worst of the road was over for that winter, and flattered me with the expectation of soon meeting with deer and other game in greater plenty than we had done since our departure from the Fort.

To Absent Friends

Robert M. Ballantyne
York Factory, 1843

Robert Ballantyne spent six years in the service of the Hudson's Bay Company. He later turned to writing and became a prolific author of adventure books, based on his experiences with the HBC. In this story from his book, Hudson's Bay; or Everyday Life in the Wilds of North America, *Ballantyne relates a lively Christmas celebration at York Factory.*

CHRISTMAS MORNING DAWNED, AND I opened my eyes to behold the sun flashing brightly on the window, in its endeavours to make a forcible entry into my room, through the thick hoar-frost which covered the panes. Presently I became aware of a gentle breathing near me, and, turning my eyes slowly round, I beheld my companion Crusty standing on tiptoe, with a tremendous grin on his countenance, and a huge pillow in his hands, which was in the very act of descending upon my devoted head. To collapse into the smallest possible compass, and present the most invulnerable part of my body to the blow, was the work of an instant, when down came the pillow, bang! "Hooroo! hurroo! hurroo! a merry Christmas to you, you rascal!" shouted Crusty. Bang! bang! went the pillow. "Turn out of that, you lazy lump of plethoric somnolence," whack!—and, twirling the ill-used pillow round his head, my facetious friend rushed from the room, to bestow upon the other occupants of the hall a similar salutation. Upon recovering from the effects of my pommelling, I sprang from bed and donned my clothes with all speed, and then went to pay my friend Mr. Wilson the compliments of the season. In passing through the hall for this purpose, I discovered Crusty struggling in the arms of the skipper, who, having wrested the pillow from him, was now endeavouring to throttle him partially. I gently shut and fastened the door of their room, purposing to detain them there till *very nearly* too late for breakfast, and then sat down with Mr. Wilson to discuss our intended proceedings during the day. These were—firstly, that we should go and pay a ceremonious visit to the men; secondly, that we should breakfast; thirdly, that we should go out to shoot partridges; fourthly, that we should return to dinner at five; and fifthly, that we should give a ball in Bachelors' Hall in the evening, to which were to be invited all the men at the fort, and all the Indians, men, women, and children, inhabiting the country for thirty miles round. As the latter, however, did not amount to above twenty, we did not fear that more would come than our hall was calculated to accommodate. In pursuance, then, of these resolutions, I cleaned my gun, freed my prisoners just as the breakfast-bell was ringing, and shortly afterwards went out to shoot. I will not drag the reader after me, but merely say that we all returned about dusk, with game-bags full, and appetites ravenous.

Our Christmas dinner was a good one, in a substantial point of view; and a very pleasant one, in a social point of view. We ate it in the winter mess-room; and really (for Hudson Bay) this was quite a snug and highly decorated apartment. True, there was no carpet on the floor, and the chairs were homemade; but then the table was mahogany, and the walls were hung round with several large engravings in bird's-eye maple frames. The stove, too, was brightly polished with black lead, and the painting of the room had been executed with a view to striking dumb those innocent individuals who had spent the greater part of their lives at outposts, and were, consequently, accustomed to domiciles and furniture of the simplest and most unornamental description. On the present grand occasion the mess-room was illuminated by an argand lamp, and the table covered with a snow-white cloth, whereon reposed a platter containing a beautiful, fat, plump wild-goose, which had a sort of come-eat-me-up-quick-else-I'll-melt expression about it that was painfully delicious. Opposite to this smoked a huge roast of beef, to procure which one of our most useless draught oxen had been sacrificed. This, with a dozen of white partridges, and a large piece of salt pork, composed our dinner. But the greatest rarities on the board were two large decanters of port wine, and two smaller ones of Madeira. These were flanked by tumblers and glasses; and truly, upon the whole, our dinner made a goodly show.

"Come away, gentlemen," said Mr. Grave, as we entered the room and approached the stove where he stood, smiling with that benign expression of countenance peculiar to stout, good-natured gentlemen at this season, and at this particular hour. "Your walk must have sharpened your appetites; sit down, sit down. This way, doctor—sit near me; find a place, Mr. Ballantyne, beside your friend Crusty there; take the foot, Mr. Wilson;" and amid a shower of such phrases we seated ourselves and began.

At the top of the table sat Mr. Grave, indistinctly visible through the steam that rose from the wild-goose before him. On his right and left sat the doctor and the accountant; and down from them sat the skipper, four clerks, and Mr. Wilson, whose honest face beamed with philanthropic smiles at the foot of the table. Loud were the mirth and fun that reigned on this eventful day within the walls of the highly decorated room at York Factory. Bland was the expression of Mr. Grave's face when he asked each of the young clerks to drink wine with him in succession; and great was the confidence which thereby inspired the said clerks, prompting them to the perpetration of several rash and unparallelled pieces of presumption—such as drinking wine with each other (an act of free-will on their part almost unprecedented), and indulging in sundry sly pieces of covert humour, such as handing the vinegar to each other when the salt was requested, and becoming profusely apologetic upon discovering their mistake. But the wildest storm is often succeeded by the greatest calm, and the most hilarious mirth by the most solemn gravity. In the midst of our fun Mr. Grave proposed a toast. Each filled a bumper, and silence reigned around while he raised his glass and said, "Let us drink to absent friends." We each whispered, "Absent

To Absent Friends

friends," and set our glasses down in silence, while our minds flew back to the scenes of former days, and we mingled again in spirit with our dear, dear friends at home. How different the mirth of the loved ones there, circling round the winter hearth, from that of the *men* seated round the Christmas table in the Nor'-West wilderness! I question very much if this toast was ever drunk with a more thorough appreciation of its melancholy import than upon the present memorable occasion. Our sad feelings, however, were speedily put to flight, and our gravity routed, when the skipper, with characteristic modesty, proposed, "The ladies;" which toast we drank with a hearty good-will, although, indeed, the former included them, inasmuch as they also were *absent* friends—the only one within two hundred and fifty miles of us being Mr. Grave's wife.

What a magical effect ladies have upon the male sex, to be sure! Although hundreds of miles distant from an unmarried specimen of the species, upon the mere mention of their name there was instantly a perceptible alteration for the better in the looks of the whole party. Mr. Wilson unconsciously arranged his hair a little more becomingly, as if his ladye-love were actually looking at him; and the skipper afterwards confessed that his heart had bounded suddenly out of his breast, across the snowy billows of the Atlantic, and come smash down on the wharf at Plymouth Dock, where he had seen the last wave of Nancy's checked cotton neckerchief as he left the shores of Old England.

Christmas ball in Bachelors' Hall, York Factory.

St. Boniface Cathedral and Grey Nuns' Convent (1858). Painting by William Henry Edward Napier.

Archbishop Taché's First Christmas in Manitoba

Alexandre-Antonin Taché
Winnipeg, 1845

Alexandre-Antonin Taché (1823–1894) was the first archbishop of St. Boniface. He was educated at the Séminaire de Saint-Hyacinthe and the Grand Séminaire de Saint-Sulpice in Montreal. In 1845, as a 21-year old novice, Taché was chosen to accompany Father Pierre Aubert on the Oblate mission to the Red River Colony. After an arduous two-month journey by canoe from Montreal, they arrived at St. Boniface on August 25, 1845. Upon seeing the young Taché, Bishop Provencher was said to have remarked, "They send me children! But it is men we need." However, Provencher soon revised his assessment. He ordained Taché deacon on the Sunday following Taché's arrival and then priest on October 12, 1845. Nearly four decades later, the Winnipeg Daily Sun *interviewed Taché about his memories of past Christmases. The following is Taché's recollection of his first Christmas in Manitoba.*

"AN ARTICLE ON MY Christmas reminiscences in the Northwest for half a century!" laughingly exclaimed His Grace the Archbishop of St. Boniface, to a *Sun* reporter. "I should be delighted to write one, but I'm not much more than half a century old myself, and I have only been in the Northwest thirty-eight years. You can therefore see the inconvenience it would be to give you the reminiscences of fifty years. But sit down and I will reply to such questions as you may ask."

"My first Christmas in the Northwest? Yes, it was in 1845—just 38 years ago. There were then about fifteen houses in what is the Winnipeg of today. Some of them were comfortable dwellings. One of them—a log house—is still standing. It was the McDermott homestead, and is located opposite the McDermott House on Post Office Street. It is a storey and half high. At the Christmas time I speak of it was occupied by Mr. McDermott and his family.

"There were some half-dozen houses on Point Douglas. The only stores were those kept by the Hudson's Bay people, McDermott and Sinclair. Yes, the church of St. John's was then in existence. So was the ladies' college. There was no Presbyterian church, nor, of course a church of any other dissenting denominations.

"On the St. Boniface side were a number of buildings, the most prominent of which was, of course, the cathedral and Bishop's palace. The cathedral was then in course of construction. There was also a good-sized school house, attended by over 100 children—girls and boys; the sexes were co-educated at that time. The younger children were taught by the Sisters of Charity and the elder ones by the Bishop and his priests.

"The first missionary in the Great Lone Land after the English conquest was Father Provencher. He was also the first Bishop of St. Boniface. The other priests here at that Xmas besides myself were Father Aubert, in whose honour Aubert Street, St. Boniface, was named, and Father Laflèche, the present Bishop of Three Rivers, Quebec, for whom a street was also named in this municipality.

"The cathedral stood just in front of the present building. It had two stone towers, with a tin belfry. As I before told you, it was then in course of construction. There was nothing inside but the bare walls, and they were not even plastered. It was as large as the present building.

"We held Midnight Mass on Christmas Day. I remember it well. It was a beautiful, bright, clear, regular Manitoba night, with the thermometer down to -30. There were no stoves in the church, and very few in the country. I also remember that some seven or eight panes of glass were broken, and there was no glass in the Great Lone Land to replace them. It was indeed a bitter, biting Christmas night, but not withstanding this the church was crowded—yes, overcrowded. I think there were almost as many Protestants present as Catholics.

"They came from many miles around. There were as many people in the parish of St. Boniface then as there are now; the parish was a great deal larger. A large number of those present came in sleighs. I should think there were 200 of them. Several of them were drawn by oxen. It was a very funny sight to see people come to Xmas Midnight Mass in a large wood sleigh drawn by oxen; but very funny things happened in those days, you know.

"The people were very thinly clad. It was a mystery to me then, and has been ever since, how they stood the cold. I could see that they suffered a good deal during the service as they kept moving their feet. But there was very little liquor in the country then and people could stand the cold better than they can now. The Mass of that Christmas midnight was celebrated by Bishop Provencher, with Father Aubert as assistant priest, Father Laflèche as deacon and myself, being the youngest, as sub-deacon.

"There was no organ in the church in those days, and previous to the commencement of the service I remember Fathers Aubert and Laflèche entertaining the congregation to a species of amateur concert on two clarionets, assisted by two half-breeds on violins. They played well, the people were delighted, and that was the first time that the music of clarionets and violins was heard in a church in the Great Lone Land. The Christmas carols were very sweetly sung by two Sisters of Charity—Sisters Lagrave and Gladu. Both had remarkably sweet voices. The former came from Montreal. The latter was a half-breed, a native of the place. Notwithstanding the extreme cold, the open windows and the absence of stoves, the service lasted over two hours. The exemplary behaviour of the thousand people assembled evidenced their deep piety."

Archbishop Taché.

Returning from Midnight Mass in Manitoba, ca. 1880.

A Red River Christmas

Joseph J. Hargrave
Red River Settlement, pre-1870

In an account published in 1882, J. J. Hargrave recalls the pre-Confederation days of the Red River Settlement and the holiday festivities that took place. Eating, dancing, and drinking were the orders of the day, as was writing letters to friends and family. The mail was a crucial lifeline to the outside world for the community, and news from abroad was always widely anticipated and welcomed.

During the period of the existence of the colony at Red River previous to its adoption into the confederation of Canada, Christmas was the principal one of the few breaks in the monotony of its yearly life. Occurring at midwinter, it marked the passage of the shortest days and formed the turning point from which the earliest anticipations of approaching spring, still four months in advance, were dimly entertained. The winter tracks on river and plain, beaten by the traffic of a widely-scattered and scanty population, would be getting into permanent trim, convenient for the passage of carrioles and cutters, containing visitors on the way to visit relatives and acquaintances, often domiciled at considerable distances from each other.

An Englishman on his first arrival in the country, would doubtless be inclined to view with dismay the vast plains over which the wintry wind whistled with unresisted sweep, and the bitter cold compelled the traveller to bury himself in furs, mittens and caps protected with ear-lappets, in order to escape from its inhospitable chill. On the other hand, the homes of the people were entirely exempt from poverty in its least endurable forms. Even the wandering Indian could always procure fuel for his wigwam fire, skins to cover him, and as a rule food to eat.

The settlers were all in sufficiently comfortable circumstances; and the Christmas week was for them a season of enjoyment after their fashion. Balls, frequently kept up for several successive days and nights, formed possibly the favourite diversion, at which the singular dance known as the "Red River Jig" was the most invariably prominent feature. Strict sobriety was not a conspicuous feature at these assemblages; or, if it could in any sense have been said to be so, it was "from its absence." Nevertheless strangers in the country, and travellers of experience in passing through it, found an interest in attending such gatherings, and generally took both an active and lengthy part in the festivities.

With regard to table indulgencies, the numerous luxuries now imported in vast quantities were entirely absent. Fruits, and the more perishable appendages of luxury, were unknown. Latterly, when capable of being stored in canned shape, they were introduced, but twenty years since even this had not been attempted. The country itself, however, then produced delicacies which have now disappeared. Game, whitefish, venison; and above all, the buffalo, with his flesh, his tongue, and his "boss," or hump, were to be found everywhere and were obtainable by everybody.

At Christmas time of course all such good things were in special request and were supplemented by a class of stimulants, spirituous and vinous, excellent of their kind. It is doubted by persons well qualified to speak with authority whether in respect to the latter class of articles the present time shows any improvement on its predecessor.

Absent friends were always warmly remembered at the Christmas season in Red River Settlement. This tendency was assisted by the fact that only a few days previously, say about the 15th of December, the dog trains bearing the packets of letters and postal matter for the northern districts and posts started from Fort Garry for Norway House. This was the opening stage of a vast and intricate system of intercommunication, by means of which intelligence passed between every station belonging to the Hudson's Bay Company situated between the Rocky Mountains and Hudson Bay, and extending north to the Arctic Sea. Its extent and importance will be understood when it is remembered it was the only event of the kind occurring during the winter season. It was the winter mail of the Northern department.

Everybody who could write made it a point to correspond with their friends by this opportunity, and hence the first fortnight of December was always a period of literary effort, the conclusion of which—as necessitated by the departure of the packet—left the mind relieved and ready to welcome the holiday season.

The packet system itself, as regards its aspect from Fort Garry, was so arranged that about the end of February the runners arrived, bringing out letters from the entire north, although, of course, only in cases of posts to the south of the River Saskatchewan could the latter be *in reply* to such as had gone out in December. In cases of the more northern posts, a letter would travel till almost spring before reaching its destination.

The arrival of these packet bearers was, of course, a great event at the interior posts. At Norway House, the first stage from Red River, the runners made it a point to pass their Christmas. This they found an arrangement as agreeable to them as to those who had for weeks previously been looking for them.

After the departure of the letters, the principal harbinger of the holidays, of a public character, was the celebration of Mass at midnight on Christmas Eve. This was always done at St. Boniface, and, when possible, by Bishop Taché himself. It formed a very singular sight. The settlers frequently, from considerable distances, came driving in their carrioles by the magnificent winter moonlight night. The lighted windows of the cathedral, which was then an almost solitary building—gleamed on the surrounding snow and the music pealed impressively on the silent night. The solemnity was usually kept up until after 2 o'clock in the morning. Communicants were numerous and for many years perfect decorum was maintained. Latterly, however, this interesting ceremony was discontinued—I believe in a great measure, because, in waiting for it, many persons were wont to find an occasion for conviviality which rendered their presence a source of disturbance to their more sober-minded neighbours.

Ever since the establishment of the Church of England at Red River in 1820, Christmas Day has been observed with religious worship. In the time of which I write Divine service was celebrated in the morning at St. John's Cathedral by the Bishop of Rupert's Land, and was attended by the settlers at least as any of the weekly services of the church.

"Manitobah"–Settler's House and Red River Cart. Painting by William Hind, ca. 1862.

The Festive Season in the Olden Days

John J. Gunn
Red River Settlement, pre-1870

John J. Gunn (1861–1907) was the son of John Gunn and Emma Garriough. His father was an MLA for St. Andrews North and his grandfather, Donald Gunn, was a member of the first legislative council of Manitoba. J. J. Gunn was married to Eleanor Flanagan, and together they had one son, who died in infancy. Gunn himself died a few months after his son in 1907, from an accident on his farm at East Selkirk.

In the following account, Gunn describes how the holiday season was celebrated in the "olden days," which he took to mean as the era before the Hudson's Bay Company transferred their territory to Canada in 1870. According to Gunn, Christmas was observed simply in those days, whereas New Year's Day was the big event of the year to which everyone looked forward.

THE REIGN OF THE Hudson's Bay Company came to an end, and that of responsible self-government took its place. With the latter came a new population, which brought with it new industries, new institutions and new customs as well. And as this population outnumbered the old so the customs and usages of the latter went out before those of the former; this at least where the two populations have mingled to any extent, though in the more remote and least progressive of the old settlements the old customs still prevail.

But it is the festive season and the manner in which it used to be observed that we have to do here. And perhaps nowhere is the difference between the new and the old more marked than in the manner of Christmas observances.

With us Christmas is the great day of the year and something special and extra must be done to mark it. We exchange gifts; newspapers issue Christmas numbers; the churches are decorated for it, and so are the markets; we dress trees for the children and, that they may not forget the day, cram their stomachs with harmful sweets and their minds with still more harmful myths, to put it mildly. All these are things of the present. In the old days Christmas was not over-observed, but neither was the day nor its significance forgotten. In the few churches that there were, appropriate services were held, that was all.

But New Year's Day! That was the day of all days in the year. With us that day is devoted to making calls and exchanging compliments. These things were also done in the olden time, but with certain peculiar features entirely unknown today. Then New Year's Day was a red letter day and it was looked forward to and prepared for days and weeks in advance. Two things were deemed essential to a proper observance of it. Plum pudding and rum. It was an unfortunate member of society who could not have these two things on New Year's Day, and no one who could have them did without. Then as now, there was an upper tendom in the land wherein fashions were set. The Hudson's Bay Company's officers were royal entertainers, and none knew better how to "celebrate" when occasion required; and down through every stratum of society their methods were copied, of course. And so all strove—and with astonishing success—to provide something good to eat and something fiery to drink, to entertain their friends on New Year's Day. Those whose taste for the "ardent" was perennial and who lost no chance of indulging at all still procured a quart or so to honour the day.

Even the Indians through the land, and their name was legion, remembered New Year's Day; none so well in fact; and long before sunrise were on the tramp, the men with their guns and the women and children with sacks or other receptacles in which to stow such gifts of food as might fall their way in a royal day's begging. It was the discharge of their "flint-locks" that usually aroused the slumberous white man on this particular morning. A visit from these people was always expected and prepared for at both farmhouse and fort; and it was seldom indeed that they were turned away empty handed.

When a party of Indians came to a house they invariably discharged their guns before entering as a compliment to those within. Another feature of their visit was that beside passing the compliments of the season and shaking hands all around, they also insisted on kissing and being kissed. From this ordeal no one on whom they could lay hands was excepted, from the host and hostess down to the baby; the man-servant and the maid-servant and the stranger who was unfortunate enough to be within the gate not even escaping.

Christmas Morning on the Red River Settlement

Anonymous
Red River Settlement, 1864

This account of Christmas morning on the Red River Settlement was published in the Nor'-Wester *newspaper in 1864. The saying, "the more things change, the more they stay the same" comes to mind when reading it. Most parents will find the chaotic scene that it describes to be quite familiar!*

HOURS PAST FROM THIS, the dear little ones below have been up and out of bed to ransack those stockings—puffed with comfits (declining of course, the usual staple of breakfasts, "just bread and butter.") They are now in the full tide of wonder and mutual display of their hordes of toys. Novices upon that noble animal, the "Rocking Horse"—have ere this clasped wildly behind at his rigid tail, clutched madly in front at the flowing mane, and finally with a yell of terror rolled from his back to look up and see the proud creature with his glass eyes blazing at nothing, continuing his untiring gallop as cool as his "Brummagem" stirrup iron. The creaking of ungreased wheels of barrows and waggons have resounded unceasingly through the house, mingling with the blended din of mouth organs, cheap accordions, drums, whistles, trumpets, watchmen's rattles and such like incentives to harmony. Flutes and violins for the youngsters, whose mothers insist "have a perfect passion for music and such an ear," have been blown into, and scraped upon, until all the nervous dogs and cats in the neighbourhood who haven't "a passion for music" have fled distractedly from the sound, leaving the tied-up "Towsers" to howl in dolorous unison.

Five times in every five minutes has the new watch been held to the ear, and opened "to look at the wheels;" once in every ten seconds have harmless coxcombs shoved beneath their eyes that "first pair of boots" and through all their talk and running and shouts and playing, the one hand has been deployed to dive incessantly into a deep pocket and fish out for the "munchers" overhead anything to be thought of from a sugar almond to a bit of "citron" stuck in and ornamented with broken pieces of almond shell of the one side and a mashed raisin on the other. Now have the new books been rushed through for the pictures and now does the big chap decide between two little ones, who are quarrelling as to which is Robinson Crusoe and which his man Friday.

Yes it is Christmas; it belongs to the children and sorrow lie at the door of him or her who deprive them of their dear prerogative or darken with a word or look the sunshine in their bounding happy hearts.

Louis Riel's provisional council, 1870.

How Riel's Prisoners Got Their Christmas Dinners

An Old Resident
Upper Fort Garry, 1869

Several dozen men were held by Louis Riel during the Red River Rebellion. Although the prisoners were well treated, their provisions were sparse and consisted mainly of pemmican. In the following story, an anonymous writer known only as "An Old Resident," recounts the efforts of some local citizens to provide a Christmas meal for the prisoners.

WHEN THE MORNING OF the 25th December, 1869 came round in Red River it found 63 prisoners in the hands of the Provisional Government of Assiniboia, of which Louis Riel was president.

They came to be there because when they were asked by a representative of Governor McDougall to take up arms for their country, they complied; but they soon found themselves deserted, and Riel finding them with arms in their hands, lodged them in jail.

He fed them with pemmican. It so happened that the Canadian Government owned some dozen or two quarters of beef. The writer, on applying for the use of this supply of meat, was allowed to use it as food for the prisoners. It could not be served raw and the only hotel in the place refused to cook it. Fortunately, the representative referred to left behind him in the village a cooking stove, a man servant, a horse and a leased house. The services of all were put in requisition and the wife of old Brian Devlin, the only baker in the place, undertook for a consideration of five shillings to bake a sack of flour, the flour being bought in the place. In this way it came about that every morning there was sent up to the prisoners two boilers full of hot tea and several loaves of bread, and every afternoon at about one o'clock, a mess of boiled beef and bread.

On the day before Christmas the writer spoke to a few friends as to whether anything extra could be added to the very plain bill of fare on Christmas Day.

All that could be done in the leased house would be the boiling of an extra quantity of meat and tea. Outside aid must be caught for the rest. George Emmerling, the owner of the hotel, professed himself willing to do what he could, but on referring to his better half was told the dinner for their own guests would tax all their capacity. At last a promise of aid was cordially given by some ladies. In one house it was resolved a plum pudding should be made; a young lady, now the wife of a Northwest magistrate, undertaking the mysterious operation.

Mrs. James Stewart lent a willing hand in the manufacture of pastry, and two o'clock the following day was fixed upon as the time at which all should be ready for despatch to the Fort, nearly three-quarters of a mile distant.

The latter part of the repast came near being spoiled by the absence of dried fruit, which at last was obtained at eight o'clock in the evening at the store of Mr. Henry McKenney, now Coolican's corner, and figuring at some hundreds per foot frontage, (the land—not the raisins).

On account of the pressure of work at the leased house, it was found necessary to dispense with the usual breakfast. As no communication had been had with the prisoners as to the intentions of those outside, they unfortunately knew no reason for the absence of breakfast, and as the whole dinner was not ready until four in the afternoon, they had all come to the conclusion that for some unknown reason they were going to go without any outside food that day. Indeed, I believe many of them stayed their appetites with pemmican before our dinner reached. At four o'clock, however, the late Joseph Crowson, with his faithful black nag, was on his way with the beef, tea, pudding and pastry, and as the darkness was settling down he was delivering his supplies to the starving prisoners, and their thanks were duly returned through Mr. Crowson to the ladies who had so kindly assisted to give this relief to their otherwise monotonous fare.

This was the way, then, that they got their Christmas dinner. It looked strange to see the sled on which the tea boiler was usually carried to the Fort. The cover was not a good fit and the jolting of the sled caused the tea to run over the edge of the boiler and in a few days a small mound of ice tea formed on the sled and daily received additions to its height.

Of the then residents of Winnipeg who were not in jail, I think there are not a dozen now in the city. All indeed, I can recall at the moment are Capt. Donaldson, Mr. Robt. Patterson, Mr. John Higgins, Mr. Wm. Drover, Sr., a few ladies and the writer.

A Notable Dinner at Fort Garry

Anonymous
Upper Fort Garry, 1870

After an arduous journey of over two months from Ontario to Manitoba, the 1,200 troops of the Wolseley Expedition arrived at the Red River Settlement in late August, 1870, only to find that Louis Riel and his followers had already abandoned Upper Fort Garry. By Christmas, the expedition's provisions were running low, and the soldiers were tired of the usual army fare of hardtack and beans. Their quartermaster came up with a unique solution just in time for Christmas.

THERE ARE THREE OR four of the boys now in Hamilton who went up to Red River in 1870, in the first expedition under Colonel Wolseley, now the distinguished hero of many fields, and commandant of the Nile expedition. The boys all took good appetites with them. The change from the pâté de foie gras of comfortable home to the fat pork of the expedition, from sponge cake to iron-clad hardtack, from caramels to white beans, from ice cream to dessicated potatoes, and from champagne to black tea, bothered some of the more delicate for a few days; but road making, stockade building, rowing and portaging, soon gave a flavour to the articles on the new bill of fare that was astonishing, and which created a wonderfully rapid reduction in the provision stores.

The pork, at first, was all good. It was made from hogs grown for the purpose, and the best of brine kept it in prime condition. The barrels of pork were heavy, and on long portages everything connected with pigs was condemned with a readiness of tongue, a force of utterance, and a red-hotness of sentiment that are peculiarly the property of the disgusted soldier. One day some genius discovered that the brine in a barrel of pork weighed a good deal. He removed the bung and the preserved brine ran out. He replaced the bung, shouldered the barrel and smiled softly to himself and skipped across the portage. The secret was told to another, and another, and another, until half the six months' supply of pork for the expedition was brineless and rusty. The officers discovered the trick, and the game was up. The weather was very warm and the tapped pork was none the better for it. Of course the brineless stuff had to be used first, and some of the dinners for a few weeks could have been smelt in Egypt or Australia.

The hardtack was great. It was harder than a reporter's cheek. One of the boys dropped a piece on a ledge of rock one day, and a prospector came that way, and found it. He broke his hammer on it, and carried it off to exhibit as a remarkable specimen of natural steel. The hardtack was hard.

For three months, seven days a week, the menu read as follows:

Pork and beans, potatoes, hardtack and tea. Or

Beans and pork, hardtack, tea and potatoes. Or

Hardtack, beans, potatoes, pork and tea.

Or

Potatoes and tea, hardtack, pork and beans.

Finally we reached Fort Garry. The country was not prepared for us. No arrangements had been made to victual the army; the pork and beans, hardtack, potatoes and tea for breakfast, dinner and supper, still remained in force. After a while the Hudson's Bay Company hunted up some old oxen that could no longer earn their living in cart harness, and slaughtered them for beef for the boys. It was tough beef. But it was fresh beef, and the boys feasted. The supply was short, however, and after the first day nobody could get enough. Only those people who have lived three months on pork and hardtack can imagine how good even sole leather beef is. The boys grumbled continuously.

In the sergeants' mess, the grumbling was loud and deep. The quartermaster sergeant was appealed to. "Get us more beef," said they, "what are you for anyway? Can't you fill us up just once?"

This grieved that good young man, the quartermaster sergeant. He felt for his fellow sufferers. And he felt for himself. On several occasions he managed, with the aid of his gentlemanly and obliging pioneers, to get the quarter of some poor old or chucked into the "taked over" pile, without the usual preliminary weighing and crediting to the Hudson's Bay Company. This was wrong. It was very wrong. But what was a poor, starving quartermaster sergeant—with about 35 poor starving sergeants depending on him—to do? These surreptitious quarters went to the sergeants' mess. But still they howled for more. And they kept howling.

Time passed. The beautiful, boundless prairie was buried beneath the snow, and the Red and Assiniboine rivers were nearly solid. It was the evening before Christmas.

At supper, the sergeants growled their usual growl about the scarcity of fresh beef and the lavish plentitude of salt pig. They no longer dignified it by the name of pork.

The good quartermaster sergeant was again grieved. But the lines of care that excessive grief had brought to his handsome face were presently chased away by a broad grin—an inward sort of a laugh. He whispered to Sergeant Hank and they put on their greatcoats, muffled up and went out into the dark and frosty night.

Next day was Christmas.

A Notable Dinner at Fort Garry

Christmas Day in barracks is the great day of the year. The sergeants made great preparations for the proper celebration of the day. The rooms were titified up and ornamented, and varnished, and fixed to no end. The wine list was appalling, and of spirits there were more varieties than ever killed a man in the older provinces. The dinner was to be a great one. Many civilian friends had been invited to the banquet, and a most stupendous time was to be had.

"How about the dinner?" asked one hungry sergeant of the quartermaster sergeant. "Are you going to give us enough to eat today?"

Benevolence flickered all over the fine face of the Q.M.S., as he replied, "Yes, me boy; today you shall not grumble. Today's dinner will be one to be long remembered. Everybody will have everything they want, and all of it they want. Don't forget it."

The dinner bugle sounded. The sergeants trooped in. My! What a spread! What a noble display of viands! What an astonishing variety! What a plentitude of everything! Beef! Beef everywhere! Beef soup, beef stewed, beef broiled, beef roasted, beef curried, beef à la everything! beef ad infinitum! beef galore!

They sat down. The face of the Q.M.S. beamed with pleasure. The good young fellow felt that, at last, he had distinguished himself. There was no longer any grumbling. Every eye shone with pleasure, every mouth watered with anticipation, and all showered compliments upon the bountiful Q.M.S.

"Pitch in, boys," shouted that personage. "What'll you have? Try the stewed beef—is it good?"

"Good? Well, we should say so. Yum yum! Betcherboots it's good!" came from all sides of the table.

"Go it, boys. How do you like the soup?"

"Haven't tasted anything half so good since I left Hamilton," said Staff Sergeant Jim as he helped himself to a juicy quarter section of roast beef.

Such a clatter of knives and forks! Such a disappearance of provender! Such uproarious laughter! Such jokes and quips, and such ejaculations of approval.

"Best roast beef I ever put a tooth in." "Capital curried beef that. Gimme s'more." "'Nother hunk off'n that joint, please."

It was a great feast and a long feast. It was the first opportunity the boys had had to make a good square meal since they left home. They said so, and they ate as if they spoke the truth. The beef was praised to the skies, and the good Q.M.S. was the most popular man in the regiment. At last the slowest—or greatest—eater had emptied his plate for the last time. All were satisfied. All looked supremely, superlatively, transcendently happy. The Q.M.S. saw his opportunity. He arose to his feet, smiled all around the board, and said:

Upper Fort Garry in 1860.

"Gentlemen, have I satisfied you at last?" Grand chorus—"You have."

"Is there one man here present who is not perfectly, absolutely satisfied?"

Grand chorus—"No, not one," and cheers.

"The dinner has been a great—a noble success?"

Grant chorus—"It has."

"And you would all like to have it repeated tomorrow?"

Rousing cheers, and grand chorus—"We would."

The Q.M.S. turned to Sergeant Hank and said: "The best thing we can do, Hank, is to go down and get the rest of that old horse!"

The sergeants looked blank for just two seconds. Then the situation dawned upon them. There were two doors to the dining room. In an instant both were crammed with anxious and escaping sergeants and civilians. They all had sudden and peremptory business outdoors.

A Christmas Ball

Mary FitzGibbon
Winnipeg, 1876

Mary FitzGibbon, who had come to Manitoba as a governess, provides a glimpse of holiday entertainment in Manitoba and the traditional custom of calling on friends and neighbours during the holidays.

SNOW LAY SEVERAL INCHES thick on the ground at Christmas, and we had sleigh-drives over the smooth prairie; one great advantage of Manitoban winters being that when once the ground is covered with snow, if only to the depth of five or six inches, it remains, and there is good sleighing until the frost breaks up in March or April. Sleighing parties are varied by skating at the rink and assemblies in the town-hall, where we meet a medley of ball-goers and givers, each indulging his or her favourite style of dancing—from the old-fashioned "three step" waltz preferred by the elders, to the breathless "German," the simple *deux-temps*, and the graceful "Boston" dance, peculiar as yet to Americans and Canadians. The band was composed of trained musicians who had belonged to various regiments, and, on receiving their discharge, remained in Canada. The hall was well lighted, the floor in good condition, and we enjoyed taking a turn upon it, as well as watching the Scotch reels, country dances, and Red River jigs performed by the others.

It was a gay and amusing scene, but the heavy winter dresses—many of them short walking costumes—worn by the Manitoban belles, looked less pretty than the light materials, bright colours, and floating trains of an ordinary ball-room. The absence of carriages and cabs, and the intensity of the cold, compelled ladies to adopt this sombre attire. The mercury averaged from ten to twenty degrees below zero, frequently going as low as thirty-three, and occasionally into the forties; yet the air is so dry and still, that I felt the cold less when it was thirty-three degrees below zero in Winnipeg than when only five degrees below in Ottawa, and did not require any additional wraps.

On New Year's Day the now old-fashioned custom of gentlemen calling was kept up, and we had many visitors, among them the American Consul, Mr. Taylor, known in the Consulate as "Saskatchewan Taylor," from his interest in the North-West and anxiety upon all occasions to bring its capabilities before the public. He came in the evening, and, following the American style, remained more than an hour, so that we were able to get beyond the conventional topics of health and weather, and found him very pleasant and entertaining.

Christmas Goods!

JUST RECEIVED.

CARDS—German, English, American & Canadian.

TOYS—In tin, wood, papier-mache, china &c.

DOLLS—Rubber, china, unbreakable, kid &c.

PLUSH GOODS—Satchels, mirrors, photo frames &c.

ALBUMS—A great variety of styles.

GAMES—Euchre, nations, authors, old waid &c.

JEWELRY—Watches, chains, earings, brooches &c.

Vases, fine Chinaware, Silverware, Clocks, Inkstands, Workboxes, Writing Desks, Gifts Books, Toy Books, Accordeons, Violins, Mouth organs &c. &c. too numerous to mention.

We charg nothing for showing goods the pleasure of doing so quite repays us.

G. W. McLAREN,

Chemist & Stationer.   MANITOU & MORDEN

G. W. McLaren advertisement, December, 1885.

Christmas at York Factory

George Simpson McTavish
York Factory, 1879

George Simpson McTavish, Jr. followed in his father's footsteps and entered service with the Hudson's Bay Company in 1879. In this excerpt from his autobiography, Behind the Palisades, *McTavish writes about Christmas preparations at York Factory.*

PRECEDING THE REGULAR CHRISTMAS ceremonies and festivities there was the bustle of preparation, chief among them being "Shop Day." For the purpose of economizing time and labour, and in accordance with the Company's system of conserving the officers' and men's wages, there were only two shop days practically in the year. the principal one before Christmas, when some of the newest goods could be had, with such little luxuries as confections or sweeties in very simple form, a few raisins and currants to give the cannon-ball grease-pudding a semblance to its civilized plum brother of happy memory. Much deliberation took place among all classes in regard to purchases, especially men with wives and children, the process of cutting out articles approaching the fine art from experience. Unlike civilized barbarians we kept within the limits of our purses, schooled our roaming inclinations to actual necessities, only relaxing Spartan discipline when Christmas, that glad time of the year, warranted an exhibition of somewhat pathetic extravagance in its very poverty of selection. Yet from these limited resources and opportunities, more genuine pleasure was derived and seen, than could be thought possible by anyone who had not witnessed wholesome enjoyment and happiness in the school of experience, where many possessions are certainly not burdensome. With everybody supplied according to the extent of their resources, and the limitations of luxuries, the arrival of Father Christmas was looked forward to with satisfaction.

The officers, however, had to face an opening ordeal of welcoming the Indian ladies and treating them to conversation sweeties, white and coloured confections with words printed on them such as "I love you" in gaudy colours, with a few muscatel raisins thrown in for variety. The ladies were dressed in printed calico, those opulent in the world displaying narrow saresnet ribbons to assist their charms. There was a concoction manufactured at the factory called Pomatum, coloured grease with a strong perfume, decidedly an adjunct to any lady's toilet. These said ladies plastered their straight black hair till all was pink, and the wind wafted their presence from afar off.

Next came the Indian men, staid and undemonstrative, in great contrast to their women, who gravely shook hands, said "What Cheer" the common seaman's salutation, engrafted in the Cree language from constant repetition and relevancy. The noble red man was content to accept, as a concession to our inferiority on this occasion, a glass of sugar beer, when another shake and "What Cheer" brought the proceedings to our public reception to a close.

Following the practical transfer of its charter rights of Rupert's Land by the Company in 1869, and owing to the rapidly increasing facilities of transportation in the development of Red River, Manitoba was created a Province in 1870, and old Fort Garry with its name changed to Winnipeg became the provincial capital marking a momentous change and epoch in the history of the Company, the head office work and surplus supplies were necessarily moved to Winnipeg, and the decadence or diminution of historic York Factory begun by the sidetracking process of Father Time.

When the reserve liquor was forwarded, a certain amount was kept at the factory, a foreseeing precaution when the Territorial Government assumed control of liquor, and it was from this source the officers received their Christmas remembrance of old customs, one bottle each of old brandy, port and sherry wine being deposited in the several rooms by Mr. Fortescue's orders on Christmas Eve. Liquors could only be obtained by permit through the Lieutenant-Governor of Keewatin, hence the well-husbanded reserve at York Factory was valued accordingly, apart from its unrivalled quality. Hudson's Bay blankets and Hudson's Bay liquors are still synonyms of that quality.

The sugar beer was a local product, the ingredients being brown sugar, hops (privately imported) and yeast. The brewing was started in September, or as soon as the supply of sugar could be obtained after the ship's arrival, so as to be ready for the Christmas treating. Watching the process of fermentation, skimming the workings or froth, etc., made anticipation of the finished product a constant joy, and fund of conversation as to its final merits. Not that we could make it deadly intoxicating, but if we could clarify it, by straining and settling, make it show a head, and taste the hops, imagination could do the rest, raising the concoction to the dignity of Bass's best. No one ever got drunk on sugar beer, and good liquor was too scarce and valuable in emergencies to be abused.

There were no "mornings after" in Hudson Bay, at the time of which I write, though in former days up till 1870, there was more or less rum rationed out to the men, to bring out any old animosities among the fighters with chips on their shoulders, who desired to start the year with black eyes and a salved conscience. Many were the stories told me by old William Gibeault of the Christmas Homeric combats, inspired by demon rum in the olden days, when would-be gladiators went outside their houses or tents, flapped their arms, and issued a challenge to all and sundry by cock-crow.

Christmas at York Factory

After church service and lunch, there might be a dog driving for diversion, when each officer or man was supposed to drive his Indian or half-breed washerwoman, as a slight token of appreciation for her valued services, to make her feel proud, so that she would continue the aforesaid valued services on another year's contract. The dogs, with gaily-decorated saddle-cloths, tinkling rows of round metal bells, carefully-attended harness, and the gaily-painted carrioles, carrying their dusky occupants encased in deerskin or buffalo robes, swept through the gates, team after team, making for the frozen river by the bull track (used in winter as a means to convey water in barrels through the ice holes, and to the factory), where racing commenced, to the cracking of whips and yells of the drivers. In the crisp cold air, one felt the exhilaration of the ozone, besides the excitement of the occasion, and another variation of the joy of living was experienced. The dogs knew that this outing was no start on a long trip with heavily-loaded sleds to break their hearts and requiring conservation of energy, so were in fine fettle. They bounded with exhilaration till the bells jingled with merriment. Everyone, human or canine was infected with inflated boisterousness. Black Care had no place in that racing procession over ice and snow, there was no room for trouble or sorrow in the glowing exuberance of Peace and genuine Goodwill. We had the whole world to ourselves, wherein to give utterance to our feelings, and the air was charged with yells, bow-wowing and laughter. Verily life was worth living in such an atmosphere of healthy happiness. Scenes or occasions like this, though few and far between, yielded pleasurable recollections, which even advancing old age with its attendant disabilities cannot destroy, but on the contrary help us to realize the compensations of less-favoured situations.

As an appetizer for a good dinner, a five or six-mile run, under such circumstances as herein narrated, cannot be equalled or surpassed. Modern cocktails cannot compare with Arctic air and exercise, and when on returning to the fort, we had given the dogs their Christmas dinner to their full content, had an icy-cold tub, a rub down with a rough towel, a change of clean dry underwear, with our best suit, and new fancy silk-wrought moccasins to adorn our outward persons, we felt prepared in every way for the great event—the CHRISTMAS DINNER.

The latest fall fresh wild-geese had been preserved in nature's storage for the occasion. There was beaver, young succulent and tender, wood-grouse—pheasants we used to call them—trout caught through the river ice, the best of lake white-fish, fried on this occasion, and browned to a turn, a haunch of fat juicy tender gamey venison, with cranberry jelly, pastry and plum puddings. nuts, raisins, and figs (if you please) for dessert, with the old seasoned port and sherry wines, whose mellowness and strength was hidden beneath a velvet taste. There was the unequalled blended tea of Hyson and Souchong, unadulterated coffee, and cigars and cheroots of exquisite flavor to soothe desire and make repletion heavenly.

Mrs. Fortescue had directed the culinary operations specially, so that Tom Wood, the steward, had not the chance to mar matters by faulty cooking.

As we crossed the seas or land, mentally, in toasting "Absent Friends" and sang "Auld Lang Syne My Dears," we were filled with solids, liquids and sentiment. What better ending than the remembrance conveyed in the following:

> "We speak of a Merry Christmas
> And many a Happy New Year,
> But each in his heart is thinking
> Of those, who are not here."

Gone are the familiar faces who sat around that Christmas table as far as I know, but the board is still spread in imagination, and they are ever present. Is it not worthwhile being able to frame such a picture of unalloyed enjoyment, mental and physical, and look at it daily? I would my pencil could have made it more beautiful, for a Christmas gathering eliminates selfishness, bringing us nearer the perfection of human attributes and aims, than at any other time of our existence.

The dinner was something more than mere gastronomic enjoyment, it was a preparation for the harder exercise in testing our further endurance at the dance which heralded a whole week's nightly rioting of the light fantastic till New Year's Day. Unconfined was that glorious dancing exhibition. Men sweated for having no petticoats or dresses, they could not hide their leg action as women could, and had to give their best in Red River jigs, Scotch reels, the Rabbit, Duck dances and old Dan Tucker. If men dropped exhausted, others took their place with a whoop of delight and derision. The only safe place for recuperation was on a snow bank outside with 40 degrees below zero, or seeking the immense tea-kettles, with lots of sugar—extravagance for this occasion only—and hard biscuits.

When the room warmed up, and the sweat began to trickle down the walls from the heated perspiring multitude, capots and superfluous clothing were discarded. Their shirts clung so tightly and wetly to the men's backs, that they would have to be torn off, to be removed, otherwise they would also have been laid aside. The women took matters more philosophically, but stayed to the end some of the belles displaying heroic continuity and fortitude in dancing with all comers.

With only a couple of hours in which to have a cold tub and sleep before breakfast, we left an experience of unalloyed happiness no one could forget. So ended my first Christmas at York Factory in 1879.

Christmas at the Averill Homestead

Emma Louisa Averill
Section 36, Township 16, Range 18, in present-day R. M. of Minto-Odanah, 1880

Cold is something that all Manitobans are well acquainted with. Early homesteaders like the Averill family had to survive through the long, harsh winters, yet they made the best of it, especially at Christmas.

THE FEW DAYS WHICH intervened after my husband's return and Christmas were spent in unpacking and arranging the many additions to our house which the boxes contained, and my husband and our guest employed their time in carpentering, for until now we had not had any proper tools, and by the time the books, writing desks and other useful, and which appear to us now, ornamental things were unpacked, some nice shelves were ready to receive them. Then we had about a dozen pictures which we put up to brighten our log walls and when all was done our room looked more cheerful and homelike than I had thought possible when we first entered it, October 13th.

The rooms upstairs were too cold to be made use of during the winter, for like a few others who were anxious to finish their houses we had put neither plaster nor mud on the rafters and the wind came in with impunity; this was a great inconvenience, as we were all obliged to live for six months in a space 20 feet by 16 feet. We partitioned off a small bedroom for myself, my sister and the children, in which we had a small stove which kept it comfortably warm; in this we now had a bedstead put and as it was not large enough to admit a second, a berth was contrived over ours for the children, being made long enough for two to sleep at each end and it answered admirably and greatly economized the room and much delighted the little occupants.

It seems a delightful change to us all to have a comfortable bed with blankets and other luxuries unknown since June, for nearly seven months we had slept on mattresses or bags filled with hay on the floor, and instead of undressing had to put on our ulsters and everything which we had to keep ourselves warm enough to sleep. My husband, my cousin and any friend had to have a large shake-down[1] on the floor of the other room, which was put aside during the day and covered with a Buffalo robe so as to form a lounge, as seats were scarce.

The weather was now very severe, Christmas morning was cold enough to make everyone contemplating a visit prepare against frost bites. We had rather dreaded this our first Christmas away from all our friends and were very glad to have an addition to our circle which was further increased by the arrival of another Englishman, whom

---

[1] A temporary bed made on the floor.

we had known slightly the previous summer and who braved Jack Frost and rode a distance of 30 miles, staying at Minnedosa the night before and getting to us just in time for dinner, which though it consisted of roast beef and plum pudding was decidedly a contrast to our former dinners on that day and alas! for the dessert over which the pleasantest hour is spent in so many homes, still the hours passed happily and we not did not despise the cup of warm tea, to which we had all become accustomed, as a beverage at our mid-day meal.

The next few days were as merry as it was possible to make them in our little house. It was too cold for any occupation out of doors beyond chopping the necessary wood and tending the cattle. In the evening we amused ourselves with Whist and other games and rarely were the lamps extinguished till midnight. The days are within a few minutes the same length as in England, but the snow being always on the ground seemed to make the daylight continue longer. The stars each night were lovely, so clear and bright, but the northern lights, though frequently visible, were not so beautiful as I had hoped to see, being colourless.

The severity of the frost must be felt to be understood; it was no uncommon thing to find in the morning our breath frozen in small icicles on the Buffalo robe under which we slept and the same on my husband's moustache and beard, yet this was a mild winter compared with the one of 1879 and though my husband would often come in and declare this country never was intended for Englishmen, he more frequently said, "Is not this a splendid climate, could anything be better?" Our thermometer was as low as 50° below zero at times, but the air is generally very still and the intense cold never lasted more than three days at a time, throughout the whole season, there were only about five days when it was too severe for the usual occupation of rail cutting.

The snow seems to come most gradually, as the whole remains on the ground from the time the first comes, which is often in October. This year it was not until November. It increases with each storm and is often four feet deep. Some weeks before Christmas our water in the well was exhausted and we had to melt snow. This at first was a tedious process, but as the snow became more closely packed, it was easy to cut huge blocks which contained as large a quantity of water and was softer and more pleasant to use than the melted ice which we tried at first, the cattle had to be taken every day to a lake about 1/2 a mile north of the house, where the ice had to be chopped out for them to have a drinking place. It was about four feet thick.

The hands and feet are the most difficult parts to keep warm. The caps which come over the ears and nearly cover the face, keep you comfortable, except your nose, which is not unfrequently slightly frozen. My husband found it most difficult to keep his hands and feet warm under the moccasins. He wore three pairs of knitted socks constantly and on his hands two pairs of woollen mitts or gloves with the fingers not divided, like infants wear, under some made of thick leather lined with lambswool. I can imagine any Englishman laughing at the idea of using his hands so encased, yet people chop and shoot in them.

In January we had some more friends to stay with us and my sister went for her first sleigh drive which she thought delightful and sometimes during these pleasant evenings we almost forgot we were in the North-West, though we were not so fortunate as some of our neighbours in possessing an American organ or other musical instrument. At this time my cousin, having taken land, left us to get logs for his house and the beginning of February my husband and sister went to Minnedosa intending to return the next day, but owing to a heavy fall of snow and strong gale of wind, they were unable to start and a concert at which my sister had promised to assist had to be postponed. When they saw that it was finer the next morning, they at once prepared for their journey and left at an early hour, which was most fortunate, as the trail had not been used since the recent snow storm and they had almost to dig their way, it frequently taking an hour to get through a drift. At 4 o'clock they were still five miles from home and one of the oxen tired out. It was not so cold as it had been, or they would have been frostbitten. To walk through the deep snow was most tiring, still they succeeded in reaching a house, where one of the sons good-naturedly brought them home with his oxen, ours walking behind and most glad I was to welcome them and find them none the worse for their tedious journey.

They had quite enjoyed their short stay at our little city and the evening before an excitement had been created by the arrival of some officers of the Mounted Police with an Indian prisoner who had been convicted of horse stealing at Edmonton. This is a most heinous crime in this country, as to deprive a man of his horses is almost as bad as taking his life, for on the vast prairie further West a man may travel for days without seeing a house. In this case it was punished by a sentence of five years penal servitude, which to a young Indian accustomed to a free roving life must have seemed intolerable. He appeared not more than 20, but such a look of hopeless misery my sister said she never saw on any face. A heavy chain was attached to one leg. The next morning when he was brought into the dining room of the Hotel to have his breakfast, which he took seated on the floor, no knife or fork being allowed him. He had already escaped twice and was now closely guarded. Captain Herbart and his party started early in their toboggans drawn by native ponies, the prisoner having to walk.

During my husband's absence I had not been at all alarmed either night, though it certainly seemed strange and lonely, but in Canada no one ever uses the bars or bolts so necessary in England; as an old man told my husband one day, everything was safe in this country, "A few years ago you might leave your hat on any part of the trail and there it would remain until you fetched it, but now there were so many English about everything got picked up." Neither are there any wild animals to disturb our slumbers. Once or twice we have heard wolves in the distance and sometimes my husband has seen one playing with our dog, but never close enough to shoot it. I believe they have been frequently shot, but I have heard of none this year. They are cowardly creatures and do not attack people. I find I have omitted to mention a party of surveyors who went last autumn to survey a township about 30 miles north of this one, we occasionally saw some of their party when going or returning from Minnedosa, and once our oldest boy went to their camp with one of them and returned greatly charmed with the novel life. In January, the camp was moved to another township only eight miles west of us. At this time, we frequently saw the chief and his assistants, which made a pleasant change from the monotony of our indoor existence. The second week in February we were one day surprised to see two of them walk in. They had burnt their tent and came for ours, and though feeling sorry for their discomfort this had occasioned them, we were always glad to see any visitors and our surveying friends were favourites with us all. The following Saturday the snow was so deep that three of them determined to come to their cache near us for some snow shoes. It was a sudden break they left the camp about 11 o'clock p.m. and feeling their way along an unfrequented trail for eight miles through snow three feet deep and many drifts, was exciting enough at first, but long before they reached the shanty where they intended to finish the night, they began to repent of their hasty decision and when after a tramp of six hours they dragged their feet to our door, they were completely exhausted and almost asleep before explaining the object of their nocturnal visit. When we saw them the next day they were apparently quite recovered and starting back in the afternoon, they accomplished their return journey much more speedily with the help of their snow shoes, which to us looked extremely cumbrous appendages, though very light ones.

The Indians at this time were catching large quantities of fish in the lakes, and bringing them in their toboggans to the different houses where they traded them for flour. At one time I believe they could be obtained very cheaply, but now they are very shrewd in making their bargains. There is only one kind of fish caught in this part of Canada. They resemble the English pike and are sometime quite large, many of the people go before the ice breaks up and through the air holes spear a quantity which their wives salt and dry. The system of trading so general in this country seems very amusing to English ways to the English people; it is one that my husband delights in and one evening a neighbour came in with a large fur cap on for which he apologized as being made by himself out of a badger skin. We admired it and my husband at once said, "I will trade cap," to which our friend replied, "All right" and putting on the cap my husband offered him settled the bargain. After relining the fur cap and binding the edges with scarlet I felt quite pleased at the exchange. The grey fur with bright trimming looked so warm and comfortable.

Spruce Boughs and Apple-Jelly Tarts

Nellie McClung
Section 20, Township 7, Range 16, near present-day Wawanesa, 1884

Food often comes to mind when reminiscing about Christmas. Nellie McClung writes about an early Christmas on her family's homestead in the Souris Valley, and fondly recalls her mother's holiday baking.

CHRISTMAS WAS A JOLLY time that year. We had spruce boughs, brought from the Sandhills, across the doors and windows, and streamers of red tissue paper and red and green balls, made from tissue paper cut in circles, folded and sewed together. Mrs. Lundy had showed Hannah how to make these, when Hannah had stayed with her in the summer holidays. Mr. and Mrs. Lundy had a store about a mile east of Millford.

I remember particularly the apple-jelly tarts that we had at Christmas and how delicious they were. The apple-jelly was bright red in colour, for snow apples were now sold in Mr. Lundy's store and Mother had used only the parings and cores for the jelly, and the other part was made into apple sauce. Mr. and Mrs. Frank Burnett, Nina and Frankie were our guests that year. A long table was set and no one had to wait for the second table. Mrs. Burnett was a pretty woman with hazel eyes and a fair skin and the most beautiful clothes I had ever seen. She had a dolman of smoke gray brocaded velvet and a black grosgrain silk dress with bugle trimming, and a gold bar brooch set with pearls, and earrings to match. She was the daughter of a well-known Montreal family and must have found the life she was now living a sad contrast to her life in the city. But she made light of the hardships of the prairie. "If only we could keep the bread from freezing," she complained once. "I cannot make very good bread anyway, but it's worse when it freezes. Even when I wrap it in Frank's fur coat, it freezes." I was not old enough to fully appreciate her gallantry of spirit but when I heard her singing to her children, "Grandpa will come with the Wo-Wo and take us away from the cold," I knew she was singing it to keep up her own spirits too.

Christmas Day has always been flavoured to me with the pound cake and apple-jelly tarts of those first days in Manitoba.

The front-room always got a new coat of white-wash on the log walls at Christmas, and everything was scoured as white as sand or soap could make it. The hand-knit lace curtains, brought from Ontario, were washed and starched and stretched on homemade frames, so they would hang straight and reach the floor. Short curtains were considered slightly indecent. The two long widths of rag carpet in bright stripes with orange warp were brought out and laid on the white floor, with the good mats, one hooked and one braided. The homemade lounge had a covering of dark maroon canton flannel and was well supplied with patch work cushions, crazy pattern of silks and satins and two log cabins, one made of "stuff pieces," the other one of prints. There were two book-cases made with spools, painted black, and set with shelves and a "what-not" of five shelves, on which stood china ornaments, a shell box, with a green plush pincushion on the top, apples filled with cloves, and cups and saucers, (honourably retired from active service because of cracks, or missing handles, but with these defects tactfully concealed in the way they were placed), coloured glass mugs, and on the top, a bouquet of prairie grasses, set in a frosted glass vase, a lace pattern on deep blue. I remember it well, for I broke it years later, when bouncing a ball, on the floor. Who would have thought a yarn ball would bounce so high?

When the weather got cold, the kitchen stove had to be brought into the big room, and it was a family grief when this change had to be made. If the weather did not come down too hard, the stove was kept out until after Christmas. Later when the storm doors and windows were added, and a bigger heater bought, a fine big barrel of a stove, with a row of mica windows around its middle, through which the coals glowed with all the colours of a sunset, the kitchen stove remained in the kitchen all winter.

But even when the kitchen stove was in the middle of the big room, there was a cheerful roominess about it. The woodbox, papered with pictures of the Ice Palace in Montreal (*Family Herald Supplement*), when covered with two boards over which a quilt was spread, made a nice warm seat and when we got the hanging lamp from Brandon, with a pale pink shade, on which a brown deer poised for a leap across a chasm, through which a green stream dashed in foam on the rocks, the effect was magical and in the pink light the white-washed walls were softened into alabaster.

Icelandic Christmas

Salome Halldorson
Lundar, 1890s

Salome Halldorson (1887–1970) was the daughter of Halldor Halldorsson and Kristin Pals-dottir, who emigrated from Iceland and settled in the Lundar area in 1887. She was born and raised in Lundar and later attended Wesley College in Winnipeg, where she received a Bachelor of Arts. Salome subsequently became a teacher and taught for nearly 20 years at the Jón Bjarnason Academy in Winnipeg, as well as at various other schools in Manitoba. In 1936, she was elected to the provincial legislature, becoming the first Icelandic woman to do so.

In the following account, which was published in Wagons to Wings: History of Lundar and Districts 1872–1980, *Halldorson recalls the simple, quiet Christmases she enjoyed as a child in Lundar.*

THE CHRISTMAS SEASON IS drawing near. It is customary at this time to bring to mind the different ways of celebrating Christmas in different lands, and it should not be out of place to consider how Christmas was spent among our own Icelandic pioneers.

At first, of course, there was great poverty in the Icelandic settlements as elsewhere and often it was difficult to reach any stores, so for either reason or both, there were few if any Christmas presents given. However, the old Icelandic custom of lighting up the room with candles was a simple and inexpensive way of making Christmas different from other times. In many districts candles were not even available in stores, so the duty fell upon the oldest boy or girl to make candles out of tallow, with grocery string as a wick. In many cases the top of a bottle was used as a mold. The wick was firmly fastened to the bottom of the mold and stretched taut at the top, then the liquid tallow was poured in and the candles carefully placed in the snow to cool.

Christmas in those days was not so much a time of merriment as it was a holy time, to celebrate the birth of Christ, the Son of God. It was a religious festival and in those times the celebration of it was simple and solemn.

Being the daughter of a pioneering family—one of the first to settle in the Lundar district—I can recall many interesting things about how we spent Christmas. And here I shall have to apologize to the readers for writing in the first person singular, though that is not usual in an editorial.

Probably the first Christmas in my recollection was one on which my father Halldor Halldorsson walked to a store kept by a man named Walton and bought a candle for each of his numerous children. We had, of course, been taught the Christmas story, but we also had heard that elves and such beings were around after dark especially on Christmas Eve (*jólasveinar*) and could be kept away by lights of various kinds, for those beings did not relish light. So we each lighted our candle, and placed it on a wooden box or some such object, and took deep joy in simply watching the light of the candle, while sitting quietly before it. If there was a picture book as a present for each of us, there was nothing more, but we were delighted. Then my mother Kristin (Palsdottir) baked pancakes (the Icelandic kind) and served them with chocolate—a special treat at Christmas. And my father had perhaps brought for us a five cent bag of mixed candy from Walton's.

On Christmas Day my father read the Christmas story from the Bible. This was called *huslestur*. Several years later when a community hall had been built by the combined efforts of the settlers, Jon Sigurdson, our neighbour and a well-known pioneer, was asked to read the Bible in the hall, and hymns were sung by the congregation without the aid of an instrument. Then we, the children, were told we should follow the example of our elders and walk up to Jon Sigurdson and say *"Thakk fyrir lesturinn."* (Thanks for the reading.)

Later still, when Johann Palsson, who owned an organ and could play it, had come to live in the community, he loaned the organ and it was transported to the community hall for the festive occasion. The service was now conducted by Rev. Jon Jonsson, a minister who lived in the district and did some farming to eke out whatever income he received for his work. Johann Palsson played the hymns and the congregation sang for the first time to the accompaniment of an instrument.

Some time later, when the community had become more prosperous, I recalled another service at which there was a Christmas tree in the hall. My father acted as Santa Claus, dressed in the usual costume. Many gifts and coloured candles adorned the Christmas tree.

In our time, when commercialism has so largely taken the place of the former spirit of Christmas, it is a relief to let one's mind wander back to those beautifully simple religious celebrations of Christmas in the early days of our Icelandic pioneers.

One of the Finest Christmas Displays Ever Seen

Winnipeg Daily Tribune, December 22, 1900

Around the turn of the 20th century, Manitobans flocked to the market district of Winnipeg to see the beautiful Christmas displays. These were displays not of holidays lights, though. They were displays of … meat. Every year, the local butchers would try to outdo one another in extravagant holiday showcases of their meats, and newspaper reporters would wax poetic about the impressive sights they saw.

WINNIPEG BUTCHERS HAVE ALWAYS been among the most enterprising class of tradesmen, but they are becoming more so every year. The Christmas display of meats in the city market this year has had no equal previously in Winnipeg and few in any other city. Indeed, a gentleman who had travelled largely in Europe and the United States was heard to declare yesterday that for quality of meat and especially beef, and taste of display, he had never seen the equal. Citizens who have not yet visited the market should not fail to do so.

Take the long line of stalls occupied by Kobold & Co. for instance; there is an exhibition of meats, the superior of which has probably never been seen. Their stalls which occupy about half of the north side of the market have been attracting great attention, not only in the daytime, but at night as well, for they have also magnificent electrical illuminations. Over their Main stall is a Union Jack studded with electric lights in the colours of the flag; at each side of the flag is a star, in the centre of which the words "God Save the Queen" appear; then underneath the name of the firm "Kobold & Co." appears. Of course the whole of the stalls are brilliant with light, there being 250 lights in all, with at least 500 flags, small and great, together with other varied seasonable decorations.

To enter into anything like a detailed description of what this firm is displaying would be too long a work and only a few of the specialities can be touched upon. There are, for instance, five enormous beef carcases—four steers and a heifer—the largest of which weighed 2,300 lbs., and the smallest 1,900 lbs. "We might have had older and large ones," said Mr. Kobold, "but our customers like meat very tender, just such as that will be." These animals were raised specially for the Christmas trade by Mr. Kobold himself. In addition to this, there are walls of magnificent carcases of beef, all fed for Mr. Kobold's Christmas trade by Mr. Watson, of Pilot Mound. One of the pretty features of the stalls is the display of mutton, which is very prettily dressed. The visitor will not fail to be attracted by it. This mutton is principally from Maple Creek, although there is also a large quantity from Prince Edward Island. Another attractive feature is a large moose, weighing nearly 800 pounds, which was killed at Shoal Lake, and there is also a bear which was recently shot at Ste. Anne, an enormous brute, weighing nearly 500 pounds. Then there is quite a curiosity for this time of the year in the shape of a "spring" lamb, seven weeks old, weighing 25 pounds; there are numerous little sucking pigs too. Another attraction is a spotted turkey. But the whole of Kobold & Co.'s magnificent exhibit is studded with interesting specimens of game, including grouse, pigeons, pheasants, prairie chickens, etc. Then there is the display of turkeys from Smith Falls—about half a carload of them. Their packed meats too are extensively displayed, but, as was said at the outset, to go into a detailed description of everything would be next to impossible and the reader would be much more interested and well repaired by a personal visit. Messrs. Kobold & Co., are undoubtedly a credit to their profession and their artistic and substantial display of meats is an evidence of the enterprise and prosperity which have helped largely in making Winnipeg what it is today.

Winnipeg's city market, ca. early 1900s. In the background is the old "gingerbread" city hall.

Postcard of Lorne Avenue in Brandon, ca. 1906.

Views of La Rivière, ca. early 1900s.

Santa Claus is a Good Lad

Gladys McKay
La Rivière, 1907

Disappointment soon turned to joy on Christmas morning for Gladys McKay and her siblings in La Rivière.

CHRISTMAS WAS THE MOST delightful time of the whole year, for I was five—and I believed, without the shadow of a doubt, in the old gentleman with the red coat and the white beard. Had I not seen him with my very own eyes at the Sunday School Christmas Concert, and one starry Christmas Eve I had heard his sleigh bells beneath my bedroom window!

That was long ago. Then, in that little Manitoba town of La Rivière, there was only one marvellous Christmas tree, and that was in the church. We had no fireplace and we hung our long black stockings on a clothes line in the kitchen.

This Christmas, while my older sister and brother still slept, my other sister and I tiptoed down the stairs. We loved the excitement and the tingle of the cold linoleum on our bare feet. Then, in the first light of dawn, we saw the unbelievable—not the expected grotesque array of full black stockings, perilously stretched over enchanting corners, and still more parcels piled underneath on the floor—not this! Our stockings hung limp, forlorn and empty! Suddenly that Christmas morning seemed dark and chill.

My older sister and brother joined us. I forgot my own bitter disappointment when I saw the tears in my brother's eyes, for he was such a big boy; he was ten, and he never cried. But all the other boys had skates and I knew how desperately he wanted skates. I thought my mother always believed if you were warm and well fed, that was the balm for any sorrow. Soon she and my father had the fire crackling in the cookstove, and with the help of my older sister, the oatmeal was bubbling in the big pot, the kettle was steaming and the breakfast table was being set.

I was always fascinated by the 'plop, plop' of the thick, boiling porridge and I would stand on tiptoe and watch for the bubbles to rise and break. This morning I listened dully; Santa Claus had failed me.

My father always seemed to believe that if you were busy that dulled the sharp edge of any disappointment so he told my brother to go and feed the chickens, and he told my other sister and myself to help him. Until now, no one had noticed his bulging overalls hanging in their place behind the kitchen stove, not long and thin like he was, but full to bursting. Just then my brother came running in, the tears still glistening in his eyes, but excitedly brandishing aloft a pair of shining skates. Santa Claus had been in such a hurry that he had almost forgotten the skates and had hung them on the door knob.

By this time, someone had found a note pinned to the overalls—Santa Claus had so many children all over the world to visit that, to save time, he had packed all the presents in the overalls, and he hoped we didn't mind. Of course we didn't mind!

Such excitement! There were treasures for everyone and it was much more fun all together unpacking overalls than each one unpacking a stocking. How difficult it was to leave those treasures and think of breakfast, but presently we were all gathered around the table chattering gaily—surely this Christmas was the best that ever could be!

My mother sat with her chin in her hands and spoke dreamily, to no one in particular. In fact, I thought she was talking to herself when she said, "Santa Claus is a good lad."

The First Galician Christmas at Bachman School

William A. Czumer
Bachman School (present-day R.M. of Brokenhead), 1908

William Czumer (1882-1963) was a graduate of the first class of the Ruthenian Training School in Winnipeg, whose goal was to train teachers for Ukrainian communities in Manitoba. His first teaching assignment was at the Bachman School District near Beausejour, where he was required to teach in four languages: English, Polish, German, and Ukrainian. He writes about the school's first Christmas concert and how it successfully integrated the different ethnicities of the students, much to the amazement of the school officials in attendance.

IN MY SECOND YEAR in the district, I decided to organize a Christmas evening in the school, the first of its kind in that area. I asked the trustees for funds and they allocated twenty-five dollars from the school budget to buy presents, candies, and nuts for the children. With this money I bought presents in Winnipeg for all the children in the school. I numbered them appropriately and during the concert they sat on a decorated table in front of the blackboard. After the concert, the children drew numbered tickets and Santa presented each with the corresponding gift on the table.

The school room was beautifully decorated with an evergreen and coloured paper chains so that everything looked festive. The concert took place the day before Christmas Eve, starting precisely at 7:00 in the evening and lasting till 10:30 p.m. The programme consisted of Christmas carols and recitations in English, Ukrainian, Polish and German. The master of ceremonies was the chairman of the local school board, a German from Galicia. So many people from the area came to this first "Galician concert" that the school room was absolutely jammed. Out of curiosity, even a few people came from Beausejour, including two English officials: the mayor and the chairman of the school board. They wanted to see for themselves what the "Galician" teacher, whom the taxpayers of Bachman School spoke of so highly, could do. They were seated as special guests in the front row.

The teacher introduced the programme by explaining the purpose of the evening, and then the programme began. The first carol "Silent Night" was sung in English by all the children. This was followed by *"Coz to proze za nowina"* (What News Is This) sung by the Polish children. Then the Ukrainians sang the traditional carol *"Boh Predvichny"* (God Eternal), and finally the German children sang "O Tannenbaum" (O Christmas Tree). Scenes from the Christmas story were acted out after each song. It was a contest of songs from four nations and the first and most unusual Christmas concert ever held in a rural school in Western Canada to that time. The obvious interest and enthusiasm of the children as they sang their native carol and the delight of the public proved how pleasing the whole thing was.

At the end of the programme, "Santa" first distributed the gifts to the school children and then the nuts and candies to all the children and adults present. There was no end to the happiness that evening. Everybody praised the children for their performance and were amazed by the teacher's inventiveness in producing such a novel programme. The teacher thanked the audience for turning out in such large numbers, the ladies for their work in decorating the school, the children for their good behaviour and performance in carolling and the trustees for the children's gifts.

The mayor of Beausejour asked to say a few words:

"Ladies and Gentlemen. I'm fifty-four years old and attended several schools in old England. I've seen many a school in Canada and have served as a school trustee for a long time, but I must confess that I've never seen such a wonderful and exceptionally interesting school as this one of yours. This evening your children and their teacher had so enchanted me that I forgot where I was. Tears came to my eyes and I had to force myself not to burst out crying like an old lady in church when the minister delivers a moving sermon.

"The whole time I was deeply moved. I marvelled at and admired the lovely arias which your children sang so beautifully. I watched the co-ordination and co-operation between all the students and their teacher, and without flattering you, because you all know me very well, I must say I never realized that Galicians had such beautiful songs.

"I still feel unnerved, excited by the impression your children and teacher made on me. Right at the very beginning of the concert, when they sang "Silent Night," which I know so well, it made me remember the Old Country, when I as a little boy ran carolling with the other children from house to house, for which we each received a penny. Not only did I remember, but I was more than amazed and admired how masterfully and melodiously your children sang that carol, as if they had been born in England. Words fail me in describing my amazement. I'm ashamed to admit that today is the first time in my life that I've ever heard Galician Christmas carols. Although I didn't understand the words, the aria spoke for itself. I never imagined you had such nice carols. But what fascinated me most was how one teacher could teach children to sing so well in four languages. For English people it is rare to know several languages. I see, ladies and gentlemen, that you have talented children and a good teacher.

"I had heard about your school and your new teacher and I was interested, so today I came down especially with a friend because there was talk in town that you would be having a "Galician" Christmas concert. On my way to the concert tonight I told my friend about your children and how two years ago I was passing by your school and they were on the road (most likely it was recess) making mud pies and throwing them at me as if they were just snowballs. I treated it as a joke, but I thought to myself that they lacked manners and discipline. Today I'm convinced that this was during the time of their old teacher, the preacher. Today all my doubts about poor discipline in your school have vanished. And I want to tell you that I'd like to see the same harmony, co-operation and organization in our school. In conclusion, I'd like to congratulate your teacher and your children for their exemplary behaviour and beautiful concert. In town I'll tell people what a wonderful school you have." Applause!

Immediately after the speech the audience sang *Mnohaia lita* (May You Be Blessed With Many Years) in unison, as if they had planned to do it. It was interesting that it wasn't only the Ukrainians who sang, but also the Poles and Germans from Galicia. The Prussians, who had boycotted the teacher from Galicia, now congratulated him and personally gave him Christmas presents. The Ukrainians, who had felt like third-class citizens in the district, stood up straight and raised their heads in pride. They were proud of their countryman. He didn't act like a "foreigner" or some ignoramus but showed himself to be in charge of the school and a leader in the vicinity, in spite of the fact that the majority of the population was not Ukrainian.

Hudson's Bay Store at Main and York St. in Winnipeg, ca. 1910s.

A World of Wonders

Ruth Walker Harvey
Winnipeg, 1900s–1910s

Ruth Harvey was the daughter of Corliss and Harriet Walker, who owned and operated the Walker Theatre in Winnipeg. In this excerpt from her memoir, Curtain Time, *Ruth vividly describes a childhood visit to the Hudson's Bay store during the holiday season. It should be noted that the store in her account is not the iconic one at Portage and Memorial Boulevard, which opened in 1926, but the original retail store at Main and York St.*

THE FORTNIGHT JUST BEFORE Christmas was a slack time in the show business and many companies planned a lay-off then. People were too busy shopping and preparing for the holidays to go to the theatre. We went shopping, too, and the very best part of it was our special trip to the Hudson's Bay Company's store.

On most of our other visits there we used one of the entrances that gave on gloves and ribbons and purses and led to the elevators. That was nice, but it was—even with a detour to the toy department—like any other big shop. On our annual, pre-holiday expedition we passed and ignored this part of the store and went to the farthest end of the building before we entered. The doors we pushed open here were like all the others, but they seemed wider and loftier and I always thought of them as "portals," for they led into a world of wonders.

To step inside there on a December day, half-blinded by the dazzle of sun on snow, was to be Ali Baba entering the vast gloom of the treasure cave. For a moment I could see only dimly the laden shelves and counters. But even before my eyes adjusted to the light my nostrils were aware of many odours—coffee, apples, warm bread, spices, tea and oranges, mingled with others pleasant but unidentifiable, in a symphonic smell of good food.

The food department of the Hudson's Bay Company's store was large, but it was not bright, obvious, and slickly hygienic as the big markets are now. It did not suggest a quick feed by fluorescent glare at an enamel-topped table in a corner of the kitchen, but rather, long feasts by candlelight at the knightly board. The dark wood in the long counters, in the high shelves lining the walls, in the ranks of cupboards and deep, mysterious bins, gave it a mellow, grand, baronial air.

Directly inside the door was the tobacco counter. In its glass showcase were pipes with bowls of richly polished bruyère or carved meerschaum, humidors and pouches, and gilt-edged playing cards. Ready, on the counter above, were tins and packets of fine cigarettes, canisters of tobacco, and wooden boxes displaying cigars like brown potentates' fingers, ringed in scarlet and gold or regally wrapped in entire robes of silver.

The counter was set just there, I suppose, for the convenience of the male customer, and it was symbolic. It dominated the place. A gentleman could step in from the street and buy his tobacco without having to make his way past the long aisles of kitchen supplies, yet in the short moment of his stay he could cast a lordly glance over the territory beyond.

And the gentleman, like a prince pausing at the door to the kitchens on a royal tour of inspection, might take one more glance at the back of the store and one sniff of the perfumed promises wafted thence and so, stopping only to clip and light his cigar, go on his way.

Well, the gentleman might leave, content with one glimpse and one whiff, but wild horses could not have dragged me out. Or even hurried me on. Mamma and I moved with leisure from section to section. We did not rush along, seizing packages and piling them into a perambulator. In due time our purchases would be sent to the house in a sleigh drawn by a horse with jingling bells on its harness. At each department we sat down on the chairs there and mamma took out her list. The clerk displayed, measured, weighed, and suggested. And while mamma considered and made her selections, I had time, leaning back comfortably with my heels hooked over the rungs of the chair, to survey the laden shelves.

One of the first sections was almost like the toy department, for the merchandise was in miniature. Here were little packets of those wonderful tastes that were spread in the sandwiches at grownups' parties. And all the things an English cook used for savouries to serve at the end of a meal instead of a sweet dessert. Small jars of bloater paste, pink shrimp, lobster, anchovy, ham and turkey. Russian caviar that did not look nice and tasted just as bad, but was exotic to think about. Sardines, invisible in flat tins, but lying there, I knew, silvery in pools of amber oil. And pâté de foie gras in shallow, yellow-glazed pots, each with a lid and a thin layer of creamy fat beneath it to protect the velvet pâté.

By this time, although I had had a sound breakfast of oatmeal porridge, bacon and toast, I would begin to feel the faint symptoms of appetite, the little languor in the stomach followed by dreamy thoughts of food. "This state," Brillat-Savarin says, "is not without its charms." Certainly I, with the visions actually before me, found it delightful and I turned to look at the neighbouring shelves.

A World of Wonders

Here were green olives, almost as big as plums, stuffed with pimientos and celery and nuts. Gherkins sweet and gherkins sour. Brown pickled walnuts. Chutneys, waiting in spiced splendour to be wedded to some princes of curries. Here were square jars of sulphur-coloured chow-chow, the kind that was very hot and very sour and that, when you spread it on bread, dripped through and made indelible stains on white middy blouses.

Here was horseradish in tall white bottles and capers in tall green bottles. Worcestershire sauce "from the recipe of a nobleman in the county." And all those other sauces the English invented to take your mind off the slabs of cold meat and the mounds of sodden vegetables. Sauces with labels that made you think of crotchety old gentlemen in London clubs and the story of the man who was blackballed from one of them and drummed out of his regiment with his epaulettes torn off, and whatever other humiliating things they do to those who disgrace the uniform, because he had taken mustard with his mutton.

A memory of last summer's sun seemed to haunt the shelves beyond, shining from the contents of the glass jars with jewel colours. Here were the jams, red raspberry and strawberry and cherry. Black-currant jam and tart gooseberry. Golden apricot and dark damson plum. Blackberry jam that was purple to see and purple to taste. Jams that made you think of English streams and hedges. And from France, precious little jars of Bar-le-Duc: currants in ruby nectar, so good to eat with Neufchâtel cheese.

And marmalades. Marmalades made in Scotland from Spanish oranges. Marmalades in small grey stone jars, brown and deliciously bitter and chewy with peel. Marmalades in big gilt tins. Marmalades made of lemons and tangerines, with the fragrance of the fruit perpetuated by sugar. Marmalades that would slide from a spoon, light and clear and flecked delicately with shreds of peel.

And jellies. Crab apple and quince glowing in their glasses, pellucid jellies "smoother than the creamy curd." Now there was a poem! The stupid person who made the illustration for it in *The Young Folk's Library* had painted Porphyro and Madeline stealing down the castle stairs, neglecting the stanza that described the best picture of all.

Oh, gladly would I sleep in an azure-lidded sleep in blanchèd linen, smooth and lavender'd, if I could wake to see what Madeline saw: the candied fruits, the jellies, the lucent syrops, tinct with cinnamon. Poor Madeline—she was bustled off by Porphyro and Keats without having had a single taste. It was outrageous.

But mamma was not so unkind. She would always buy a jar of preserved ginger, a squatty blue Chinese jar bound and looped with raffia. And some honey—the pale golden syrup that would taste of clover and prairie roses, or one of the exquisite combs that made you feel wickedly destructive when you first broke into them, thinking of the long, precise industry of the bees.

Behind the next counters were glass-fronted bins of rice and beans and dried peas. There were coffee beans and green and black teas in enormous storage canisters. And little tin and lead caddies of tea scented with lemon or jasmine that the clerk lifted down reverently from the shelves.

Beyond were the cheeses. Huge cartwheels of yellow Canadian cheese and smaller disks of white cheese made by the Trappist monks in a prairie monastery twenty miles away—the kind Schumann-Heink liked so much. Silver packages of snowy Neufchâtel and Maclaren's, orange, soft and mealy, packed in blue-white china jars. Here were green-veined Roqueforts and Gorgonzolas, looking geological from their long sojourn in the caves, chubby red Dutch cheeses, and English Cheddars and Stiltons.

It was a Stilton that papa had used for his great experiment. He had bored holes in it, filled them with port wine, and set the cheese away on a high shelf to ripen. Just after that we had all left on a month's holiday. When we came back mamma took one step inside the kitchen door and stopped. "Something," she cried in a Mrs. Siddons voice, "has died here!" High and low we searched for a carcass. We found nothing, and mamma sent for a carpenter. He traced the smell to the long pantry. "A rat," he said, "under the floor." He was just ripping up the first of the floorboards when papa strolled in and took one deep, enraptured sniff. "Ah," he said, "I believe my cheese is exactly ripe."

At the back of the store were the poultry, fish and meats. Here we passed the red salmon, the finnan haddie, the mammoth rib roasts of beef and saddles of mutton, to contemplate the plump geese and capons. Sometimes we toyed with the idea of having one at Christmas, just for novelty, but we always ended by ordering a turkey. There was nothing like a big, high-bosomed turkey for Christmas dinner. Turkey and all the trimmings for the far-from-home theatre people who might be our guests. I let mamma decide which bird to choose—it could be admired later as it browned and glazed in the oven and filled the house with a gust of fragrance at every basting—and I went on to the bakery department.

The good things that went with English tea were here: scones, crumpets, muffins, Bath buns. There were round loaves of cottage bread, each with a baby loaf on its back, like duck-on-a-rock. There was the mealy brown bread papa liked. Sometimes he would take two slices of it with an apple to the office for his lunch. He would always exhibit this small package, making a great show of his austerity. And it did seem like a meager lunch—until you remembered that he had had fruit and oatmeal and buckwheat cakes and maple syrup and sausages and coffee for his breakfast.

Next to the new-baked goods was one of the best departments of all: the biscuits. Here were the everyday biscuits and the special-treat biscuits. The bins behind the counter held the ordinary ones: social teas, fig newtons, oval arrowroots for the nursery, raisin biscuits and ginger snaps. But on the shelves above were tins of plumcake and shortbread from Edinburgh, and boxes and boxes of the very finest biscuits from England. They were packed for the colonies: boxed in tin and soldered tight against heat and cold and damp. From England they went by ship over the globe, to all the big red splashes on the map and all the tiny red pinpricks dotting the blue expanses of the oceans. To Chesterfield Islet, to Bulawayo to Simla, to Singapore. Every moment, I knew, of my day and night, it was tea time some place or other in the Empire. People were warming the pot, measuring the tea leaves, pouring on the boiling water, and perhaps while the tea steeped, opened a box of biscuits like these.

It was fascinating to open one. Under the snug tin cover the box was sealed with another sheet of tin that could be cut with the tines of a fork or with a little opener that sometimes came with the box. When you tore off this tin wrapping and lifted the thick sheets of waxed paper beneath it, there were the biscuits. Little rounds and ovals, squares and diamonds. Some shaped like coronets or like beehives. Some filled with fondant. Each sort separated from the others by paper frills as crimped as the ruffles of a regency dandy.

To us in Canada they were delicious, the best of their kind. But to Britishers in the remote outposts they must have been more than a good product. At tea—the best and the most English of all English meals—it must have been pleasant to have them. For though the strawberries might be missing, the Devonshire cream and the crumpets, here, at least, were the English biscuits, as crisp and fresh as if it were home.

England had done handsomely by her brewers and her soapmakers: they had been wafted up to the peerage as if on clouds of lather and froth. But I felt keenly that these bakers had served the Empire even better, and I hoped there had been some biscuit barons in the honours list on the King's birthday.

As we had almost circled the store now, we came to some of those things whose scents had greeted us when we entered. Here were barrels of apples, crates of oranges and tangerines, and brown Spanish casks full of grapes packed in crumbled cork: malagas as cool as jade, and great hothouse clusters that were deep purple beneath a frosty bloom.

Here, too, were the dried fruits, the raisins, currants, cherries, citron and angelica for the Christmas cakes and puddings. Mamma had bought her supply of these on an earlier expedition, and our Christmas cakes had been made. Everyone in the house had stirred a wish into them before they were put in the oven to bake for hours. Then, for two or three days they had stood on trays in the pantry while juice from preserved cherries and plums were poured over them and allowed to soak in. Finally they had been bathed in brandy and now, blanketed under an inch of almond paste, they were dozing boozily in the fruit cellar.

Today we would buy clusters of table raisins to nibble and almonds and walnuts to crack lazily at the end of dinner, when appetite had changed to a feeling of obesity, but the hand was still moving automatically to the mouth, *allargando*, like a metronome running down.

Here, too, we ordered our Christmas candies and it was hard to choose. There were bright marzipan fruits, *langues de chat* in flat boxes, silver-wrapped sweet chocolate tied with bright ribbons, yellow twists of barley sugar, butterscotch wafers and rum toffee. Dangling from a wire hung above the counter were the red-and-white peppermint canes for the Christmas tree, and small plum puddings looking like fat friars in their brown or white cloth sacks. In *Mother Goose* there was a rhyme about a king "who stole three pecks of barley meal to make a bag pudding." It must have been larger than these for:

> The King and Queen did eat thereof,
> And all the court beside;
> And what they did not eat that night
> The Queen next morning fried.

Like mush, I supposed. It made the family life of ancient English royalty seem so cozy, and I longed to taste one of these little puddings. But mamma scorned them because they were boiled instead of steamed. For our own pudding she bought here a set of good luck charms: a ring, a thimble, a threepenny bit, a donkey and a four-leafed shamrock.

And then we came to the most festive and exciting of all these special holiday things: the crackers. Some of them were magnificent, with gilt or silver trimming on the coloured crêpe paper. Some were decorated with artificial flowers or tinsel butterflies for the ladies to pin on their dresses or wear in their hair. But that was only the outside. A small label on the end of each box told what was inside the crackers: caps, charms, fake jewellery, conundrums, jokes or epigrams. Sometimes there were several prizes in each.

Oh, what delight—before the turkey was brought on—to find your cracker! What excitement to pull it with your neighbour, getting your fingers firmly on the snapper and making a terrific bang! And then the unwrapping, the unfolding of the paper caps that might be crowns or baby bonnets. And after the caps were put on, everyone read the joke or the riddle he had found. The epigrams were cribbed from Voltaire and Lord Chesterfield, and sometimes the riddles were pedantic. I remember one that sounded as if it had been made up by some waggish don: "Why is a misogynist like an epithalamium?" But most were better suited to the varied ages of a Christmas family party. Merriment would dent two dimples high in my little cousin's cheeks as she read hers: "Why does a sculptor die a horrible death?" "Why?" we would all ask, and shout with laughter at the answer: "Because he makes faces and busts!"

When we had chosen our box of crackers we came to the last stop: the department where the wines and liquors were sold. These shelves had a regimental look, with the bottles all in line, shoulder to shoulder, like soldiers on the parade ground. They were not, I thought, so beautiful as the shelves of jellies, for here dark glass often hid the colours of the wines. And my palate was too young to appreciate the contents. But as mamma ordered, the names took on an aura of festivity. First, claret for the holiday dinners. Even the children would have a few drops of claret in their glasses—enough to make the water a faint pink and to make us feel regal. Then brandy, to put around the pudding and set alight. And sherry, to serve to callers and to put in the grownups' pudding sauce. Children had lemon sauce, but at about twelve years it was possible to graduate to a small helping of the grownups' nectar, silky smooth with eggs, heavenly sweet with sugar, and divinely fiery with sherry.

And now mamma asked for rum. That was for past Christmas, for New Year's Day. It would go into the punch bowl with brandy and lemons and sugar and spices and hot water. New Year's Day was a grand day, the end of the holidays but the beginning of something new. The first page of an unread book, promising and mysterious. You began it with a fine feeling of virtue; exalted by resolutions to practise the piano more than one hour every day and sternly to conquer the Latin gerund and gerundive. Of course, you would not have to start this until the next day: New Year's Day was too busy. The close family warmth of Christmas expanded now to include all old friends, in laughter, joviality and a confirmation of fellowship. From early afternoon until well into the evening all the men in town went on a round of calls. They paid their respects to the Crown at the Lieutenant Governor's official reception and then went from house to house of friends where the women were ready with their dining tables spread with sandwiches and cakes and tea and coffee and punch. When I saw the bottle of rum on the counter I thought of the fine smell our punch bowl would have. And I thought of Mr. Barley.

For as long as I could remember I had seen Mr. Barley on New Year's afternoon. He never patronized me when I was little or was archly teasing when I was in my early teens. He talked to me just as he did to papa and mamma, and at six, at eleven, I looked forward to his New Year's call.

He was a small, slender man and the years did not change him much, except that he grew more frail and his blond hair and moustache paled with the white hairs in them. As he grew older he came earlier and stayed later at our house. He had not the strength to make the usual great round of calls, and year by year death made its cancellations on his calling list. So, sometimes as early as two o'clock the bell would ring, and when I ran to the door and opened it, Mr. Barley would blow in like a stray brown cocoon on the gust of below-zero air. I would take his beaver coat, his fur cap and his gauntlets, and we would settle him in an armchair by the fire with his punch. He would wrap his fingers about the mug to warm them. His hands were slender and the veins showed green-blue on the pale, freckled skin. He would sniff the punch, and smile, and sip.

"Very warming, very fortifying!" he would say contentedly. Then, lighting the first of a chain of cigarettes, he would talk about the theatre and the shows he had liked. He would tell us about his reading, his latest phonograph records. He had a love for French writers and French music.

"That fellow Anatole France!" he would shake his head in admiration. "You'll enjoy him when you are old enough. And that fellow Verlaine!"

He would tell us about a new song, singing it more with the left hand that sketched the melodic line than with the breath of a voice that chanted the words:

> Le temps des lilas et le temps des rose est passé,
> Le temps des oeillets aussi . . . .

And then, while we were busy with other callers, he would take a cat nap, waking for a little more punch and more talk . . . .

So the clerk wrote the order, set aside the bottle. "Hudson's Bay Company . . . Rum . . . Overproof," it said on the label—a bottle of New Year's Day! Old friends and their greetings, pleasant talk, laughter, fruitcake, a fine feeling of virtue, and dear Mr. Barley, and that fellow Verlaine.

Mamma checked her list. Yes, with the rum, everything was ticked off. She folded the slip of paper and put it away in her purse. I buttoned my grey lamb coat, tightened the red wool sash around it, and pulled on my mittens. Now I was impatient to get away. I felt as if I had walked around the world, and the little languor in my stomach was a pang of starvation. As I hurried mamma to the door, I would look up at the coat-of-arms. The little fox had a smug look, I thought, as if he had just licked his chops.

Turning Back Memory's Happiest Pages

Verena Garrioch
Portage la Prairie, 1900s–1910s

Newspaper columnist Verena Garrioch recalls Christmases from her childhood in the early 1900s–1910s in Portage la Prairie. Her story was first published in the Winnipeg Tribune *in 1957.*

CHRISTMAS IS A TIME for remembering. The pudding is made, the cranberries cooked, the presents wrapped, and the turkey waiting to be stuffed. The tree is up and the lights turned on. No matter how blasé we may think we have grown, there's something about their warm glow that melts us.

Our thoughts turn backward. And because that silver star on the top of the tree is symbolic of the story of the Child in the lowly manger, it is natural that memories recalled are those of happy childhood Christmases. It is likely the smallest gifts were the most treasured possessions of our childhood, the sweetest memories the most simple ones.

The Gifts

Perhaps you remember especially the first pair of ice skates and hockey boots; the first long sleigh with a certain kind of runner and steering gear—like the kids across the street had. Or maybe it was a certain doll for which your mother and older sisters had made a most beautiful wardrobe. You recall the fun you had dressing it up for a party, bundling it up for a winter outing, with even a velvet hat and a muff, too!

And there was that first big humming top; the wonderful kicking donkey. And remember the store! Cardboard partitions unfolded, slid into position and there were tiny little boxes and jars containing various things sold in a grocery store. There was a tiny tin scoop and miniature tin scales, and you were the shopkeeper and the other kids came to buy. Mimicking the man in the store where your mother shopped, you assured your customers "this is the very best brand of tea in all the world."

The Ribbons

Girls will remember how they liked to get hair-ribbons. There were the school days when it was the rage to see who could have the biggest hair bows, the widest, stiffest ribbons—red ones, green ones, plaid ones.

I invented a special box for mine. There was a round stick on which the ribbons were wound. This winding pressed out some of the creases. Holes in each end of the box kept the stick in place. A slit in the top of the box let the end of the ribbon poke out. Each day, for many days in a row, you could unwind a different ribbon to wear to school. When the box was empty you wound the ribbons back on and started all over again.

And there were all the wonderful new games you got for Christmas presents. Nicest thing about them was that around Christmas time Aunties and Uncles and other Christmas visitors took time to play games with you. Everybody laughed and had fun, children and grown-ups as well.

The Story Game

There was Snap, Old Maid, Tiddlywinks, Parcheesi, Peter Coddles. This was a "story game." There were cards with words or phrases printed on them, and a little booklet telling how Peter Coddles went to New York, the experiences he had there, and the presents he brought home to his family. One person read the story and as he paused at the blank spaces the players took turns filling in the words from the cards they held. And you laughed loudly when it turned out that the cards said "Peter brought his wife the best gift of all, an old overshoe, for his mother-in-law a bunch a sour grapes, and for the baby a hippopotamus."

It's fun remembering those games you used to play. When you were a little older there was checkers, dominoes, croquinole and Pit. Pit was a card game. You traded on the market, wheat, oats, corn, barley and rye. You yelled that you wanted to trade two, three or one card, and when you got the whole set you yelled, "corner on wheat!" Wheat was the highest and you scored 100.

And remember how all the family played games at Christmas parties, like blind man's buff, or, blindfolded, tried to walk up to the picture of the donkey on the wall and pin his tail in the right place. And there were charades, musical chairs, button-button, who's got the button, poor pussy, black magic, and many others.

Staying Awake

Remember the year you tried to stay awake to see how Santa Claus landed on the roof and got into the house? Ours was a flat, tin roof that used to make a heck of a row when it rained or hailed. I actually had to hold my eyeballs up trying to keep awake until I could hear the reindeer land on the tin roof.

I never heard anything—except my mother and older sisters come upstairs and say what was to go into whose stocking. But I wasn't disappointed I didn't see any reindeer because before my fingers got tired holding up my eyelids I heard I was getting most of the things for which I had dropped hints to Santa.

Santa Was There

I hope quite a few other Manitoba youngsters got the thrill I had in believing that once St. Nicholas made a real flesh and blood pre-Christmas visit to my house. We weren't supposed to come in the front door when we had been playing out in the snow, but for some reason I did, this day, and there was Santa sitting in the living room talking to my father.

He was plump, had twinkling eyes, round cheeks and a long white beard. The few moments of wild delight at seeing Santa sitting on the sofa were short lived.

It WAS the longest, whitest, nicest beard I'd ever seen, but our visitor was Most Rev. Samuel Pritchard Matheson, Archbishop of Rupert's Land. Oh, well, my thrill about Santa Claus was wonderful as long as it lasted. Christmas is a good time to remember these things.

Farmer's Supply Co. advertisement, December 1916.

Christmas at Asessippi

Arthur R. Devlin
Asessippi, 1915

By Christmas of 1915, the First World War was well under way, with Canadian troops seeing their first combat action in the spring of that year. Arthur Devlin recounts the Christmas concert of 1915 in Asessippi and how it was to be the last for many of the young men in attendance. It was also to be one of the last for the town itself. Asessippi was already in decline by the turn of the century, having been bypassed by the CNR, in favour of Roblin. The town no longer exists.

This story was first published in the Manitoba Pageant *in 1974 and is reprinted courtesy of the Manitoba Historical Society.*

THE CENTRES OF THE whole community at the time were the church and the school. The church was located at the bottom of the Asessippi hill near the bridge, across the Shell River, leading to the store, boarding house and grist mill.

For weeks the school teacher, Miss Sadie McLennan, and some of the parents, had been working on the Christmas concert program. The decorations for the church and tree were homemade; real candles were used for lighting, which were a fire hazard unless handled very carefully. Coloured paper flowers and streamers were made by the ladies and actual cash outlay was very small.

All the school children were involved in the program of singing and pageantry. A good deal of arguing went on as to whose child should play the lead part, and who should have the lead in the singing. The teacher had to be diplomatic to a certain degree, but she was capable of laying down the law when necessary.

The young men from the surrounding area were nearly all in uniform, having joined the 226th Battalion of Canadian Infantry; conscription had not come in yet so they were all volunteers. The draft came later taking men from the German and Galician settlers, few of whom had volunteered as most of their parents had come to Canada hoping to escape such things.

On the night of the concert, sleighs, cutters and jumpers hauled by one or two horses arrived at the church in the valley. They came from an area of ten to 15 miles around. The stable of the church held only eight horses, so the others were blanketed and tied in the bush all around the church. The lights were now on—a few coal oil lanterns hung outside and oil lamps inside. These smoked and fluttered every time the door opened, but nobody seemed to mind, partly because they did not know any differently.

The preacher, Rev. McLean, had arrived from Shellmouth. Asessippi was one of the four churches where he conducted a service every Sunday, using a good team of horses with a buggy in summer and a cutter in winter. He was usually invited for dinner by a farmer or the village people. This of course included feed for the horses.

The concert started about 7 p.m., led by the local choir singing, with Mrs. Adams at the organ. This was followed by the school children putting on various scenes from Bible stories.

Many of the local boys in uniform were there sitting with their girlfriends and some of the young couples got married before the men left home. Because transportation was slow at the time, they had no hope of getting home on leave.

It was a festive occasion, one of the highlights of the year, and yet much different from other years. Many people did not realize and would not for some time, just how serious was the occasion. Many of the men left the next day, never to return.

These concerts always started with the singing of "O Canada" and closed with "God Save the King." On this special occasion the reeve was called upon to make a speech; the names of the young men who had enlisted were read out, and special mention was made of several who had left early in 1914, at the call of rally to the Empire. Some of these were remittance men who left England to come to the colonies as settlers, a few were family "black sheep," but most of them were good, capable men, just a little green to our Canadian ways.

After the concert program, presents were handed out to the children by Santa Claus (one of the robust local men), then coffee and sandwiches were provided by the women—no charge.

This was one of the last real Christmas concerts in the area. Many were held in later years, but not attended as well, due to war conditions, and most of these were sad occasions, with announcements of local residents wounded or killed in action. Some of the girls had also gone as nursing sisters, or into the cities on war work.

Driving home after the concert, some people went to local parties. Those with children usually went straight home, but not always; often there would be a room set aside at a farm house for a nursery with eight or ten children asleep. However, all the farm people had to be home in time to milk their cows at six or seven a.m. daily, since most of them relied on their cream cheques for groceries.

Thus passed the Christmas of 1915, a great contrast to life in the same area today.

Thinking of Home

Charles Douglas Richardson
Somewhere in France, 1917

Being away from home at Christmas is never easy, but for soldiers fighting in the trenches in World War I, it was a particular hardship. Originally from Saskatchewan, Charles Douglas (Dick) Richardson enlisted with the 4th University Company, Princess Patricia's Canadian Light Infantry (PPCLI) after he graduated from the Manitoba Agricultural College. He went overseas in the spring of 1916. Just after New Year's, 1917, he wrote to his friend Edna Chapman, a fellow MAC student who lived in Ninga, a hamlet located between Boissevain and Killarney.

Dear Edna:-

MY LETTERS TO YOU lately have contained apologies for not writing regularly and this one promises to be no exception to the rule. I can say though that I have neglected others also, most of them worse than I have neglected you, so you see what a poor correspondent I am getting. I forget whether I wrote to you from the Base or not. I remember mailing a Ronelles Camp Magazine to you however. I really don't know whether there is anything in it that would interest you but I thought it might give you some slight idea of the lighter side of camp life.

Well, you see I am back again and have been for more than a month now enjoying life among the things that are most interesting to the world in general. I was up in the trenches for a couple of good long spells and am just writing this in a hurry to get it away before I go in again.

Since coming here I have had one letter from you dated Oct 29th and needless to say I have read it several times and enjoyed it immensely. My mail has gone all to the dogs lately for having moved at a busy time, my parcels and letters that were meant to reach me for Christmas have not shown up. They have gone to Shoreham I expect and then—well the mystery deepens. My mother and sisters and several other people have mentioned various things they have sent but I am still waiting for the evidence to arrive that I may thank them.

Oh, I do enjoy your interesting 'lingo' as you seem inclined to call it and you may write just as much of it, as often as you wish.

I am afraid that during the winter at least, I shall not be able to write as often as I have done for it is almost impossible to write under conditions that are not as congenial as they are during the summer months but I shall do my best. You may be sure I shall not forget you for I value your friendship very highly. We are spending three-fourths of the time in the trenches now, so our rests in billets are short and if it were not for so much polishing of brass and buttons it might be sweet.

I have not reached the 'fed-up' stage yet. Perhaps after the next five years of the war I shall probably have had enough.

It is hard to realize the change in the battalion since I was here seven months ago. There is only one left in my platoon who was here then, and it is a rare thing to meet a familiar face from the 4th Univ. Co. But such is life!

Crawford is here but has left direct connection with the battalion and is now on the brigade staff on special work. He has been through a good deal of experience since I left.

I wonder if I shall have a chance to meet Merril over here. It will only be a chance but if you let me have his address it may be that sometime I shall be billeted near his battalion and then I shall be glad to look him up.

I hope you had a very pleasant Christmas. I know it would be different with your thoughts more than ever centred in the 'Beautiful land of Normandy' but I think you may rest assured that the boys over here are looked after so generously and lovingly by those at home that their Christmas and New Year festivities were more than they ever dreamed of under the circumstances.

Christmas Day was spent much the same as any other with me for I was in the trenches then, except that Fritz and we exchanged greetings in so friendly a manner that would have opened the eyes of peaceful Canadians. I don't think it would do to go into details.

Your news of the M.A.C.[2] brings back memories. Whiting and I were talking last night about the old times we had there. Do you remember Whiting? Perhaps you do not, as he was in the Second Year when I was in the 5th.

I left England just a week or two after the 196th arrived there and I was not able to see any of the boys in it. Ramsay wrote me from London when he was on leave. By the way I can't seem to find out where his brother Bill is. He was on one of the other companies of our battalion but I have not been able to find him since coming back. Jenkins has also kept out of sight. I don't know whether he has been wounded or not. I must make a special effort to find out.

[2] Manitoba Agricultural College

Thinking of Home

So you still think you would like to be a nurse do you? Well, you are a plucky little girl. I think I told you once, I should love to be wounded if you were my nurse, and I can repeat the same statement with added emphasis.

I am sure you felt quite dignified when you presided over the Red Cross Society meeting among all the old ladies and schoolmarms. I should like to have come in about that time, but I must compliment you on your ability to make them come through with their two 'bucks' membership fee.

Since you mentioned that a Chaplain writing in the *Christian Guardian* was describing the battle of June 2nd I was wondering if it was Mr. Fallis. He was at a clearing station back of the line where I was taken and he was doing everything possible to make the men comfortable. There were hundreds lying on stretchers when I got there waiting for dressing by the medical attendants and this Mr. Fallis, who is a friend of our family, was taking cocoa around and sending messages to relatives of any of the boys who wanted them sent. When he came to me he did not recognize me—I suppose I was not quite as rosy as usual and besides I had two weeks growth of beard on my face—but he asked me my name and where I came from and from that time everything was cheery. I know he writes for the *Christian Guardian* quite regularly.

Well, my little friend, I must close. You always say not to make any excuses for scribbling but this is simply terrible.

Don't forget that I am always a willing recipient of cheery, breezy news. They have a flavor of prairie freedom that I long to enjoy again in reality. I shall write just as often as I possibly can, and you may be sure there are many times I would write if I could but it is not so easy just now.

Here's hoping for Peace in 1917!

As ever, sincerely

Dick

Three months after this letter was written, Lance Corporal Richardson was killed in action on April 9–10, 1917 at Vimy Ridge. He was 25 years old.

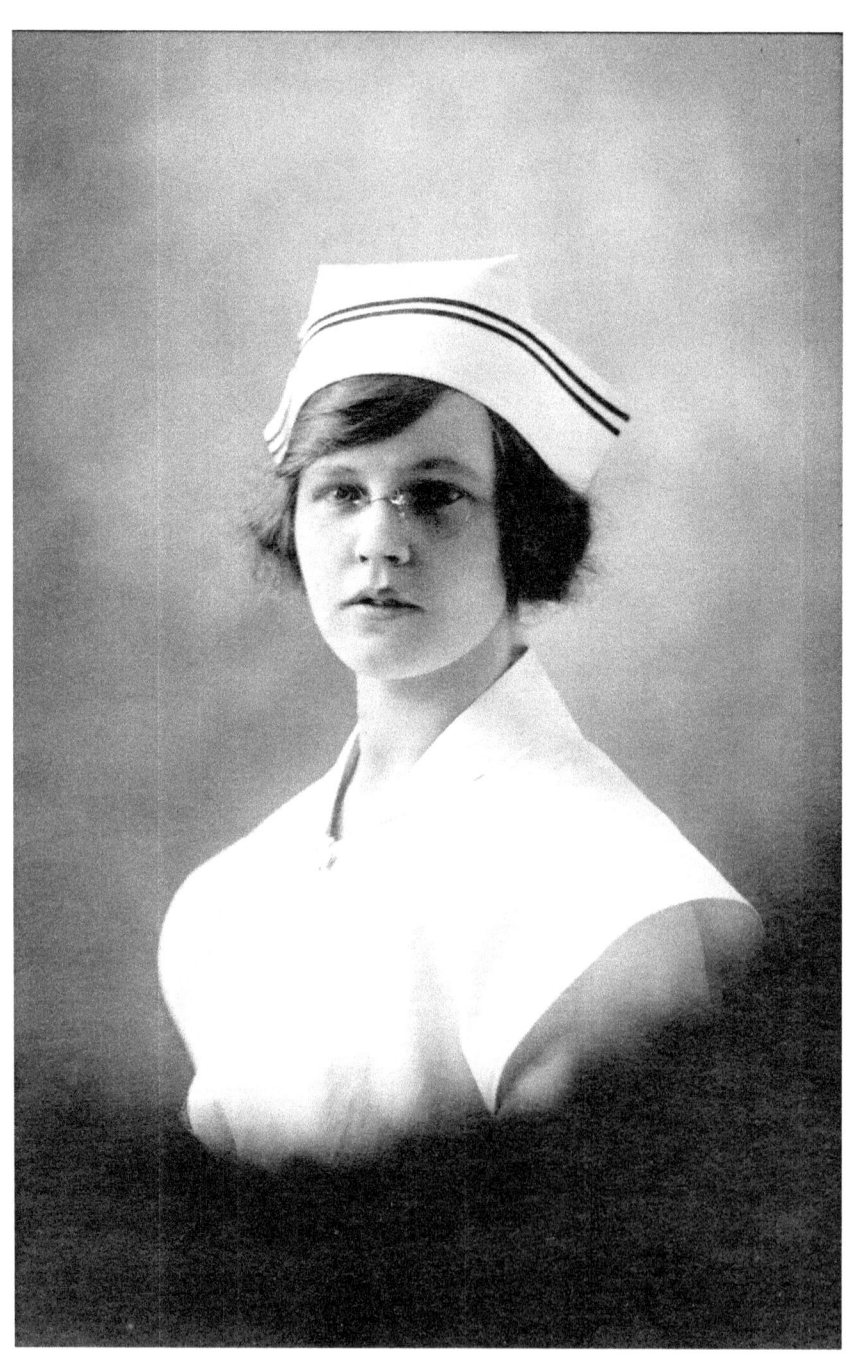

Evelina Adams (née Sinclair).

The Spanish Flu Comes to Neepawa

Evelina Adams
Neepawa, 1918

Just as the world was recovering from the Great War, it was hit with the Spanish Flu pandemic. Manitoba was no exception. By January 1919, there were nearly 13,000 cases in Winnipeg alone, and over 800 people had already died. Nurse Evelina Adams spent her first Christmas away from home tending to the sick in Neepawa.

EARLY IN NOVEMBER THE first cases of Spanish Influenza began to appear. An Isolation Hospital was opened in a fairly large two storey building, owned by Mr. James Dempsey, situated on the north corner across from the Hamilton Hotel. I do not know who was in charge when it opened. The place was closed for a while and re-opened early in December. Dr. McGinnis, the health officer, asked for a nurse from the hospital to take charge and I was chosen. Two Neepawa girls volunteered to help. They were Robeena Fusee, a teacher whose school was closed at Vista, Manitoba and Kathleen McGinnis, the Doctor's daughter. We were considered to be under quarantine with no one allowed in. We were busy, mostly routine cases. One shattering experience was a man brought in from a work camp up north, very ill and delirious. After a terrible day and night he died. This was our only death, fortunately. Two patients, the McConachy twins, Bill and Don, were admitted following the death of a brother at home. While ill they were quite manageable, but during their recovery one never could be sure of what caper they would be up to. We were very relieved once they were discharged. Christmas Day loomed, we were not very busy so the girls were allowed to clean up and go home. Christmas Eve, my first away from home, lonely and scared as well. A livery stable was right back door, and everyone drove horses and sleighs in those days. The hotel, with a beer parlour, was across the street with so many men celebrating. When they started for home, the noise and language left me rigid. The girls from the hospital brought a parcel to the door from my home Christmas Day and the Mayor of Neepawa, Mr. McKay himself, brought me a fine Christmas dinner. The "Flu House" closed early in January and I arrived safely back in the hospital dead tired. Miss Wood had me put to bed in a single room, and I slept all one night and the next day.

School classroom decorated for Christmas concert, ca. 1915.

Christmas in a New Canadian School

Mabel E. Finch
Fraserwood, late 1910s

School Christmas concerts are featured in several stories in this anthology. The Christmas concert was often the most anticipated social event of the year, particularly for rural communities. It was not unusual for the entire community to be involved in the preparations for the concert, with local people volunteering to build the stage sets, create the props and costumes, and to provide food for the event. Mabel Finch describes one such concert in Fraserwood in the late 1910s. Her account was first published in the Grain Growers' Guide *in 1920.*

WE WERE INVITED TO attend a Christmas entertainment, and there was to be a real Christmas tree. No, not the kind of entertainment in which you have often shared. Just wait till I tell you. This was a unique celebration—the first Christmas concert in a New Canadian district. Think of it! Actually 84 pupils, Ruthenian and Polish children, all waiting the final moment when they should step upon the stage and display their recently-acquired talents.

Excitement filled the air, mirth bubbled over, anticipation glowed on every child's face as we stepped off the train at Fraserwood. The villages and stopping places along the 60 miles of our northward journey from Winnipeg had all been very quiet and business-like but not so here. Children surrounded us on every side, children's voice piped away merrily, willing volunteers offered their services, and almost before we knew it our luggage was being borne speedily onward down the street. I thought I must be mistaken as to the size of the town and looked around to view the children's homes, but they were nowhere to be seen. True, there were a couple of houses, a store, a station and two schools besides the teachers' residence. "Then whence all the children?" I asked of Miss Stratton, the primary teacher who was piloting us along in the direction of her home. She smiled as she replied, "Oh! We dismissed school at 3:30 and asked the pupils to return at seven o'clock, but few went home. They are so excited over their first Christmas tree that suppers have been forgotten." "Poor kiddies!" thought I, "still two more hours to wait for the tree and not even a slice of bread and butter." But they gave me no reason to pity them, for their voices were full of cheer as they raised them in trilling melodies while they waited outside the schoolhouse.

Mary, a pretty little dark-eyed maiden, opened the door of the teachers' residence, and then for the first time we had a glimpse of Miss Stratton's and Miss Inslie's home. A dear little four-roomed cottage, the picture of coziness, and with an air of real home-yness that is only imparted where the true spirit of companionship reigns. A dining table, with the snowiest of linen and a tempting supper spread, a glowing kitchen fire with a full woodbox awaiting to add its contents to the flames, two bedrooms with the prettiest of embroideries and dainty curtains. A veritable oasis in a desert. What a revelation to these little Russian boys and girls, and what an opportunity for them to become acquainted with a true Canadian home. And here was Mary, who had been taken under the kindly wing of the two teachers for the night so she would be saved a five-mile journey to her home after the joys of the concert were over. Quite content and noiselessly she moved about, filling the tumblers on the table with water and putting a few pieces of silverware in place. "What a wonderful training she is getting," thought I, "why these teachers are regular missionaries."

But hark! What is that? I was left alone as I thought, to remove my wraps when I was greeting with "Hello! hello!" I swung around. No one was there. I looked again and then what should I behold but a lovely green and red and yellow mottled parrot staring at me, the newcomer. "How-do-you-do?" said Polly. "How-do-you-do?" I replied, and our acquaintanceship began. After that Polly sat at the table with us and I learned of her history and what a pet she was with the New Canadian children.

By 7:30 the crowd had gathered, the school doors were swung open and the first time the children beheld the Christmas tree in all its glory, weighted down with welcome gifts and sparkling decorations. Quickly the seats became filled, children were everywhere, children by the dozens, children by the score. Then came the young people who had only seen four or five years of their teens, and the married couples who were a few years their senior. Some wore their head shawls and entered meekly in a most unobtrusive manner, others had wool caps, toques or tams, and wore an air of greater freedom. All were intent on the tree or on the children in their prettiest garments, who were moving about with a long pent-up eagerness. The seats did not nearly accommodate the crowd, but the children taking part in the performance gathered around the platform and stood in long lines, others filled the aisles, while many of the men stood at the back, till finally about 200 people waited anxiously for the opening words of the chairman. Mr. Marck, who presided, was one of their own people and most ably filled the position. When the meeting was called to order he asked Mr. Stratton, the founder and official trustee of the school, to address the gathering. All listened attentively to his interesting talk to the young folk and then to the parents, in which he told them the purpose of the meeting and how we all aim to be one in Canada and keep our days of celebration together. Mr. Marck interpreted the address to the adults who were unfamiliar with our tongue, and then with smiles and good humour all were ready to welcome the opening chorus. Lustily 60 voices rang out in the National Anthem, while the audience stood, as is customary in our own schools, and the parents who were familiar with the words joined in the refrain.

Then followed, "O Canada," "Christmas Morning," dialogues, recitations, solos, duets and motion songs, all performed with eagerness and great ability. It seemed marvellous that children with only 11 months of English training had already mastered the language so well and were confident enough to perform in public.

As the pupils stepped to the platform we had a splendid opportunity to observe them. How manly the little lads held themselves, and how upright they stood while the girls took their places in front of them. How pretty the little girls looked with their white summer dresses or cozy woollen frocks. Frocks hanging down to their toes? Why, no. They were now Canadians and though they wore them a trifle longer than some of our wee folk, yet it was surprising to see how smart the majority of them looked. They had dainty pale pink and blue sashes and bows of corresponding colour for their hair, they had long, fair ringlets that had required many a mother's skilled foresight, hanging over their shoulders. Others again had their hair cut in buster style and tied with a perky butterfly bow of rose or blue. One almost wished their shoes had been lighter so their little feet would not have been unnecessarily burdened, but then felt shoes were cozy and warm, and that spells comfort on frosty days. How well they all kept step as some 30 marched around in a patriotic drill, winding in and out the intricate mazes, forming twos and fours, and finally concluding with "The Flag Song," where every loyal-hearted child sang, "This Is Our Flag, The Flag For Which Our Fathers Died." And these New Canadians meant the words they uttered with such force and revered the colours they so nobly displayed.

The program contained all the features of one of our programs. Why should it not? for two of our best Canadian teachers had trained the children. The sweetest of voices sang "I Don't Want to Play in Your Yard," "No Sir," and lullabies. The Topsy Turvy Drill brought forth peals of laughter as heads bobbed down behind the curtain and feet protruded above, the merry voices still singing strong though apparently the children were standing on their heads. Three numbers only were given by Canadian children, two by tiny tots beneath school age, who exhibited remarkable talent, and the hugs from the New Canadians which followed their recitations, showed that each tot had found a place in the hearts of the others.

Santa had not forgotten the Fraserwood pupils either, for after ten numbers of the program had been rendered a telegram was handed in saying that Santa was on his way and sparkling eyes showed untold pleasure. But bright eyes were changed to sad ones when the next telegram arrived with the message that Santa's sleigh had been broken almost beyond repair and he feared it would necessitate a postponement of his visit. At last a third telegram came with the good news that Santa would soon appear, and all was laughter again. A little New Canadian girl and boy had scarcely finished making their graceful speeches to their teacher, Miss Stratton, who was leaving the district, and presenting her with a parting gift, a fountain pen, when bells were heard and Santa appeared shaking his head and greeting all merrily. Huge bags of toys were deposited and then excitement was tense as every child stood and watched eagerly to see if he had been remembered. Fortunately everyone's name was on Santa's list, each little girl hugged to her heart a doll, and each boy some real boy's toy, a train, carpenter's tools or engine. Gladly Santa had filled his pack from the benevolent hands of the Young People's Society at Stonewall, and the Christian Endeavour at Virden, and carried these gifts to the homes of the needy. Hearts responded with feelings of love and gratitude to the unknown benefactors. After the toys, candy bags were distributed to all the tots, and Santa drove away with a merry farewell message, the children all wishing him a happy goodnight and safe journey to the next Christmas tree. Cozy wraps were then bundled around the sturdy New Canadians, and with a goodbye and Merry Christmas to all the school door closed, and the happy citizens sped homeward, cherishing pleasant memories of their first Christmas celebration in their new homeland.

Advertisement for W. F. Hartwell in Swan Lake.

Santa and His Marvels Come Back to City

Winnipeg Evening Tribune, November 17, 1928

The Eaton's Christmas parade in Winnipeg was a much anticipated annual event. Newspaper ads would run days in advance, reminding everyone of Santa's imminent arrival. In 1928, his Toyland entourage featured a giant caterpillar.

"Tum, tum, tum, te, te, tum," went the drums of the Toyland Band at 8:30 o'clock of this morning, saying as loudly as they could "Santa Claus is coming."

And with that the Toyland parade of the T. Eaton Company Limited moved out from "I don't know where" to the corner of Redwood and Main, and started its march through the streets of the city.

Throned in a castle of frost and ice, just to make Winnipeg kiddies feel that winter and Christmas were in the offing, Santa Claus made his triumphant march down the city streets.

Rosier Than Ever

Rounder and rosier and happier than ever, Santa came with his promises and his smiles to greet Winnipeg kiddies ahead of Noël time. His was the last coach in a parade of floats and Toyland folk that left every kiddie that saw them agape with pleasure and wonder.

First came the Toyland band, spick and span, and with their brasses glinting in the sun. Then came the funniest clowns that ever the eyes of Winnipeg kiddies beheld and—wonder of wonders—Mother Goose's rhymes ten times as large as life and just as natural.

There was a mouse big as a dog running up and down the clock; Pussy in the Well, but not getting very wet; Jack Spratt and his wife and a platter that had been licked so clean you could see your face in it were riding along.

Humpty Dumpty sat on a wall so high you couldn't see its top.

Giant Caterpillar

But, most amazing of all, a giant caterpillar came squirming down the street with terrible eyes rolling and tail swishing to a chorus of awed "O-ohs" from the wee bystanders. He was at least 10 yards long and had a hundred feet to go on.

If it hadn't been for a smile that went from ear to ear anyone would have thought him the 1928 cousin of that ancient monster of the fens, Grenfel, come to avenge himself. But that smile quelled the fears of the tiniest tot. He went beaming like a well-fed baby and just wriggling with delight to be in Santa Claus' procession and on his way to Toyland.

Friendly Mice

Even the mice were friendly. White mice and brown mice, walking on their hind legs and playing with pussycats on the way, frisked about the very jaws of the giant caterpillar.

Clowns that had been through the experience of Alice in Wonderland and stretched and stretched until their heads were yards away from their feet, capered among the tiniest horses that ever pranced through the streets. One man walked every foot of the way on his hands, and another—a clown, mind you—kept losing his head and picking it up at every other step. Elephants and monkeys and all that company of story-book animals that could be spared from their own peculiar occupations were there as well.

In all, it was a parade that not a kiddie in Winnipeg should have missed. Nor did very few of them.

Eagerly Wait

All up Main St. and down the highways and the by-ways eager little watchers held their posts from early morning until the parade came by. Santa Claus had planned his parade to take him to the doors of hundreds of boys and girls.

He could not bear to think of cold noses and colder toes meeting him, but kiddies didn't care. They waited and waited and loved Santa all the more when he came.

The only sad moment was when he disappeared into the T. Eaton Company's store not to appear again until Monday morning.

Announcement for Eaton's Santa Parade in 1928. Winnipeg Evening Tribune, November 16, 1928.

SANTA CLAUS HIMSELF

"Here is Santa Claus fresh from the frosty land of legend, smiling his greetings to the kiddies of Winnipeg as his parade passed down the streets to the T. Eaton Company's famed Toyland. Santa Claus brought up the rear of the finest parade of Toyland folks ever seen in Winnipeg." (Winnipeg Evening Tribune, November 17, 1928).

Little Girl's Wish Brings Santa to Hudson's Bay

Winnipeg Evening Tribune, November 23, 1928

Not to be outdone by their rival, the Hudson's Bay Company's new flagship store at Portage and Memorial Boulevard decided to have a live Christmas show four times a day in 1928, featuring a story about toys coming to life after a girl's wish comes true.

OYS THAT CAME ALIVE at a good little girl's wish stayed alive to delight hundreds of boys and girls by their revels when they welcomed Santa Claus to the Hudson's Bay Company's Toytown this morning.

It was no secret to the boys and girls of Winnipeg that Santa Claus was coming to Toytown today. A special showroom had been built on the fifth floor for him to greet his little friends and they were there bright and early to see him. But it was the toys' own secret how they broke the spell of ages, which allows them to come alive only at the stroke of midnight, and quickened at the little gnome's touch today. Perhaps Santa Claus carried a special magic in his bag which made the huge old clock chime twelve when he liked. Or perhaps the little girl who believed in Santa Claus and wished his company of toys alive was the wonder-worker.

Dance of the Toys

She came tripping to a stage where toys sat prettily in their showcases keeping knowing eyes upon Toytown's fireplace. No sooner had she wished—out loud—to see the toys and Santa Claus than Santa Claus's own handmaiden summoned the little Green Gnome. Tumbling head over heels, he came to her feet and got a certain message. Then he danced and twirled away into space again.

Swift as the wind he must have sped to Toyland for in less than it takes to tell it the toys came dancing on. There was a tall drum-major of the Toytown band; dolls so gorgeously gowned it made one gasp; darling Dutch dolls with real wooden shoes; Bolsheviki dolls with songs on their lips and lightning feet; a captain of artillery; a bold sailor lad, and a pair of dancing dolls that had been marked down for a bargain.

Clown's Capers

A great funny clown fooled with a big box in the corner and the lid flew open.

A Jack-in-the-box popped right out into the centre of the stage, and, like a boy in mischief, the clown ran away. But the Jack-in-the-box, who was out of the box, danced and rolled all about the stage as if he had been used to all the space there was.

Fearful that the dolls, who came trooping back to sing again, should find him, Jack-in-the-box frolicked away leaving his box behind him.

The company of toys danced and sang until the eager eyes of Winnipeg's kiddies were tired and little necks were sore with craning.

Down the Chimney

Then the closed front of the fireplace flew open and a little bunch of thistledown blew out. A sweeter fairy never trod the wind. The tiniest tot sighed with delight and was quiet while the fairy floated about the stage telling in the silent language of dancing toes that Santa was on his way.

Three lovely dolls, clad in beautiful old world clothes, came forth and while they stepped a stately measure the jingle of reindeer bells was heard.

Sliding down the chimney, puffing and blowing, came St. Nicholas himself.

"Hello, Santa Claus" a chorus of toys yelled with joy and the kiddies of Winnipeg took up the cry "Hello, Santa Claus."

Never a merrier fellow was seen. Santa Claus was as glad to see his toys alive and his boys and girls of Winnipeg happy as they were to see him.

This first appearance at 10 o'clock was only the first of many he will make. He will come back four times a day all next week to be sure and see every girl and boy there is here.

Next Stop, Pine Falls

Vera Fryer
Pine Falls, late 1920s

Vera Fryer remembers a Christmas when she and her brother were trying to get home to Pine Falls, but missed the last train before the holidays.

HE TRAIN FROM WINNIPEG to Pine Falls made a leisurely journey in the late 1920s. Over the frozen wastes of the great muskeg it would creep, cautiously, stoically, as winter took charge.

Christmas vacation! Our boarding schools closed, my brother and I were making our way to Union Station, homeward bound to Pine Falls. A blizzard was coming on as we clutched suitcases and bundles, and ran the last lap, for we were late. Catching that train was imperative; there would not be another until the day after Christmas, and there was no other way home. Hurry, hurry, ... to the gate, ... to the platform ... But what was the official saying? The train had left! Gone without us. Horrors! What to do?

"Get a taxi," suggested the man. "Drive to East Selkirk. It should be easy to get there before that train."

But how were we to pay for a trip that far? We had less than ten dollars between us. Then entered the good spirit of Christmas. He quickly grasped the horrid facts, the desperate need. Ushering us into his cab, he whisked us out of town. The blizzard was raging now; a white-out hid most the landmarks. Not a train was in sight. Ghastly fears mounted. But our Christmas spirit kept going.

Suddenly, East Selkirk railway station appeared. No, the train had not arrived yet. The station master prepared to stop it for us. We gave our tiny offering to our benefactor, and the taxi sped away, the genial driver calling, "Don't worry, I'll get more fares on the way back."

After a leisurely wait in the cozy shelter, we heard that magical wail, and saw the headlight coming through clouds of steam and whirls of snow. Safely aboard, tickets collected, we headed over the frozen swamps, through the white forests and rocky outcrops of a familiar country.

Off the train we jumped into the waiting arms of a frost-fringed parent, then into the sleigh's warm rugs and away behind the steam-clouded horses along the four mile bush road. Home, to wood stoves, coal oil lamps, Christmas tree, delicious aromas, and the enveloping love of family and home.

Winnipeg At Christmas

In Winnipeg at Christmas
    There's lots and lots of snow,
Very clean and crisp and hard
And glittering like a Christmas-card
    Everywhere you go;
Snow upon the housetops,
    Snow along the street,
And QUEEN VICTORIA in her chair
Has snow upon her stony hair
    And snow upon her feet.

In Winnipeg at Christmas
    They line the streets with trees—
Christmas-trees lit up at night
With little balls of coloured light
    As pretty as you please.
The people hurry past you
    In furry boots and wraps;
The sleighs are like a picture-book
And all the big policemen look
    Like Teddy bears in caps.

And oh! the smiling ladies
    And jolly girls and boys;
And oh! the parties and the fun
With lovely things for everyone—
    Books and sweets and toys.
So, if some day at Christmas
    You don't know where to go,
Just pack your boxes up, I beg,
And start at once for Winnipeg;
    You'd like it there I know.

—Rose Fyleman

How "Winnipeg at Christmas" Came to Pass

Wayne Chan

WINNIPEG AT CHRISTMAS IS a poem that is instantly recognizable to many Manitobans. It was memorized by generations of schoolchildren, and to this day there are still many requests for the words to it. Some know that the author was an English writer named Rose Fyleman, but how did a Londoner come to write an iconic poem about a Canadian city in the middle of the prairies?

The key to the mystery is a woman named Jean Macdonald, who had a front-row seat to the creation of the poem. In fact, she was with Rose Fyleman on the day it was inspired. In 2004, at the age of 94, she told her story to Terry MacLeod of CBC Radio. The following account is based on that radio interview, which has been re-aired by CBC several times since 2004.

Rose Fyleman (1877-1957) was an English writer of children's books, noted for her poems about fairies. In December of 1929, she was invited to come to Winnipeg as a guest speaker at a couple of women's clubs.

One day during her visit to the city, Fyleman and Jean Macdonald, who was a member of one of the women's clubs, were having tea at the Hotel Fort Garry when it began snowing outside. Upon seeing the gently falling snowflakes, Fyleman expressed a desire to go for a walk. After putting on their coats and scarves, they left the hotel and began walking west down Broadway Avenue. Hearing "Jingle Bells" being played in the distance, they came upon an outdoor ice rink filled with skaters. The Christmas music was coming from loudspeakers around the rink. Across the street, Macdonald directed Fyleman's attention to the statue of Queen Victoria on the grounds of the Legislature. Fyleman excitedly dashed over to have a closer look at the statue, which was covered in fresh snow. Just then, they heard the sound of bells and saw an Eaton's delivery sleigh pass by, drawn by a pair of hackneys.

Continued on next page ⟶

Macdonald and Fyleman turned north and walked to Portage Avenue, where they saw two policemen wearing buffalo coats, which were standard issue back then. When Macdonald pointed them out to Fyleman, she said that she couldn't imagine how they could possibly catch anyone wearing those huge coats!

Winnipeg postcard, ca. 1910s.

Returning to the hotel, Fyleman immediately sat down and grabbed a pen and paper to jot down her thoughts. According to Macdonald, Fyleman wrote six words: "snow," "Victoria," "rink," "skate," "sleigh," and "policemen." These few words formed the raw ingredients for the poem that came to be titled, "Winnipeg at Christmas," which was published very soon afterwards on New Year's Day, 1930 in *Punch* magazine.

Jean Macdonald's only regret was that she didn't come up with the idea herself. As she said to Terry MacLeod, "I could kick myself from here to Plum Coulee that I didn't write it, I tell you!" But it was a wonderful episode in her life that she never forgot. "I had many a good Christmas, but that Christmas with this experience of meeting this lovely English lady, that has been a memory that I will take with me to the very last snowflake."

Riding the Rods

Joseph Payjack, Jr.
Winnipeg, 1931

During the Great Depression, many people travelled from place to place looking for work by hopping on freight trains. Joseph Payjack, Jr. recounts the memory of one such young man, who showed up at the Payjacks' door on Christmas Day. This story was first published in Sunny Side Up: Fond Memories of Prairie Life in the 1930s *by Eileen Comstock in 2001. It is reprinted with the permission of Fifth House Publishing.*

I WAS TOO YOUNG to recall this experience on my own. You know how kids are swept up by the excitement of Christmas. However, my mother, four older sisters and a brother, as well as other family members, confirm this story.

We lived on Higgins Avenue in an area of Winnipeg still known as Point Douglas. Higgins is an avenue running east and west on the south side of, and parallel to, the CPR main line. Our house was about three blocks east of the CPR depot and the now long-gone CPR Royal Alexandra Hotel. Point Douglas was a decent but far from affluent neighbourhood, at that time feeling the effects of the Great Depression. On Christmas Day, 1931, we were preparing to have our dinner. Our family, also harshly affected by the times, somehow was still able to lay out a truly festive table—turkey, root-cellar vegetables, preserves, and traditional Ukrainian fare. The house was full. Not only our immediate family but uncles, aunts, and cousins were there to make it a true family affair.

There was a knock at the door, and my father answered. A young boy, perhaps eighteen years old or so, stood before my dad and asked for a bite to eat or a few cents. Without hesitation, my dad asked the boy in and immediately made him feel comfortable and at ease. He had a way of making people feel welcome, and so I have learned, was generous to a fault.

Dad proceeded to help the boy clean up, for he had just gotten off the freight train. He had been "riding the rods" as it was termed—a common occurrence in those days. The young man was given a clean shirt, and, a short time later, our guest came downstairs to join our family for dinner. He spent the night on the chesterfield and in the morning, after breakfast, my dad rounded up some spare warm clothing, packed a lunch with Christmas leftovers and, I was told, also gave him an undisclosed amount of cash.

Three and a half years later, on June 24, 1935, my father passed away from pleurisy. He was thirty-eight years old. This I remember well. He was well-known and well-liked, and needless to say it was a large funeral.

One day, a few years later, my mother answered a knock at the door. The man facing her smiled and said hello. Mom thought he looked a bit familiar but couldn't place him. He asked if he could see Mr. Payjack. When Mother told him of my dad's passing, the man broke down and wept openly. Regaining his composure, he told my mother that the gesture of kindness displayed that Christmas in 1931 not only helped save his life, but it was a "stepping stone" to a new beginning. He offered my mother a sum of money, but she would not accept it, even though she probably could have used it. She just said, "That is the way my husband would want it to be." The young man left and we never heard from him again.

Train hopping, ca. early 1930s.

A Vignette of a Winnipeg Winter

Eileen Wilson
Winnipeg, 1933

The following is an excerpt of a story that Eileen Wilson wrote when she was a Grade XII student at Rupert's Land College (which later became Balmoral Hall School). Her story paints a vivid picture of the four seasons in 1930s Winnipeg. I have reprinted the winter part of it.

WINNIPEG TO ME IS a series of pictures. Indeed, in looking back, we find we look on life as a series of pictures. When we think of a certain incident, we do not think only of the incident but frame it in a picture. If we think of the enjoyable Christmas dinner we had, we do not say to ourselves: "First Emma came with Jim; she went upstairs and took her things off, and then came down and joined Jim, who was having a cocktail with Father. While they were on their first, Jane arrived by herself because Frank was just putting the car away. Then came Frances and George and then Martha and Hugh. When they had all had their cocktails, we went into the dining-room two by two, Father and Mother leading;" and so on. Instead, we see them all seated around the table laughing and joking, all looking full of good cheer and feeling their best; the noble turkey, which Father is carving, and Mother at the other end overjoyed to have all the family together and looking so well. Or else, you see them later on, when people have dropped in; some are dancing, some grouped around the piano singing, others talking quietly, and all looking as if they were thoroughly enjoying themselves. It is, therefore, in pictures that I would depict Winnipeg.

Imagine for yourself a cold winter's day. The snow is falling, making everything dazzling white, and we are standing, though not for long, in front of the Parliament Buildings. The golden boy is a dark shadow up high amid the lazily drifting snow which quite out-dazzles him. The Parliament Buildings look mellow and the yellowness of the stones contrasts pleasantly with the dazzling snow of the sunshine and the soft purple-blue of the shade. The snowflakes are feeling comfortably lazy—not the mad frantic rush of yesterday with its exciting races with the wind, and pause to gaze in the windows and marvel at the feverish and tiresome existence of man. Queen Victoria sits on her throne with a soft fluffy wrap around her. After all, she is "a very little lady" and rather old. People are scurrying here and there only half visible in the glistening atmosphere, and where they have trodden they leave soft pinkish indentations and, perhaps, a cheery word, both of which are soon covered by the snow. From neighbouring chimney-tops arise leisurely curls of pink smoke. All nature is calm; but alas, we poor mortals can hardly appreciate nature at forty degrees below.

Manitoba at Christmas

Now it is night and we are travelling in a car along Portage Avenue and rapidly leaving Main Street behind us. Overhead is a canopy of twinkling lights, forming a Milky Way the length of Portage. On either side are spruce little Christmas trees all decked in blue, green, red and yellow lights. Still farther, on both sides are the shop windows dressed in their best and beaming a welcome to all who pass. There are many, for it is the night before Christmas and there are many belated parcels to deliver. We soon find ourselves on the Crescent, which is thronging with cars all sounding their horns as if we were dumb animals and that the only means of expressing our exuberance. There are many cheery words sent out into the friendly air, and the banging of doors and joy of happy laughter. The brave little trees and wreaths keep vigil outside, and attempt in their own way to do their bit towards cheering our hearts and rejoicing our eyes. Finally, we return home to be greeted with a gleam of delight by our own valiant tree.

Portage Avenue in Winnipeg, ca. 1930s.

Upon a Midnight Clear

Margaret Laurence
Neepawa, mid-1930s

As one of Canada's most acclaimed writers, Margaret Laurence needs very little introduction. In her story, Margaret reminisces about her family's Christmas traditions when she was growing up in Neepawa, and in particular, the last Christmas before her father died. Upon a Midnight Clear *was first published in the collection of essays titled,* Heart of a Stranger, *in 1976. It is reprinted here with the permission of Penguin Random House and the estate of Margaret Laurence.*

I WOULD BET A brace of baubles plus a partridge in a pear tree that when Charles Dickens wrote *A Christmas Carol* no one wanted to identify with Scrooge, before he became converted to Christmas. How very different now. One is likely at this time of year to run into all kinds of people who view themselves as the Good Guys and who actually try to make you feel guilty if you celebrate Christmas. "It's become totally commercial," they virtuously say. "*We* don't have anything to do with it."

All I can reply, borrowing a word from Scrooge, is *Humbug.* Sure, okay, the stores may less-than-subtly put out their Christmas displays immediately after Halloween; the carols may be used to advertise fur coats or washing machines; the amount of phoniness surrounding Christmas in our culture may be astronomical. But Christmas itself remains untouched by all this crassness. It's still a matter of personal choice, and surely it's what happens in your own home that counts. In our house, Christmas has always been a very important time.

My background and heritage are strongly Christian, although I reserve the right to interpret things in my own way. In my interpretation, what Christmas celebrates is grace, a gift from God to man, not because deserved, just because given. The birth of every wanted and loved child in this world is the same, a gift. The birth of *every* child should be this way. We're still frighteningly far from that, but maybe this festival can remind us. Christmas also reaches back to pre-Christian times—an ancient festival celebrating the winter solstice. *The Concise Oxford Dictionary* defines solstice very beautifully—"Either time (summer, winter) at which the sun is farthest from the equator and appears to pause before returning." For countless centuries, in the northern lands, this time of year was a festival of faith, the faith that spring would return to the land. It links us with our ancestors a very long way back.

Manitoba at Christmas

Christmas when I was a child was always a marvellous time. We used to go to the carol service on Christmas Eve, and those hymns still remain my favourites. "Hark the Herald Angels Sing," "Once in Royal David's City," and the one I loved best, "It Came Upon a Midnight Clear." It couldn't have been even near midnight when we walked home after those services, but it always seemed to me that I knew exactly what "midnight clear" meant. I had no sense then that there could be any kind of winter other than ours. It was a prairie town, and by Christmas the snow would always be thick and heavy, yet light and clean as well, something to be battled against and respected when it fell in blinding blizzards, but also something which created an upsurge of the heart at times such as those, walking back home on Christmas Eve with the carols still echoing in your head. The evening would be still, almost silent, and the air would be so dry and sharp you could practically touch the coldness. The snow would be dark-shadowed and then suddenly it would look like sprinkled rainbows around the sparse streetlights. Sometimes there were northern lights. My memory, probably faulty, assigns the northern lights to *all* those Christmas eves, but they must have appeared at least on some, a blazing eerie splendour across the sky, swift-moving, gigantic, like a message. It was easy then to believe in the Word made manifest. Not so easy now. And yet I can't forget, ever, that the child, who was myself then, experienced awe and recognized it.

We always had the ceremony of two Christmas trees. One was in the late afternoon of Christmas Day, and was at the home of my grandparents, my mother's people, at the big brick house. There would be a whole congregation of aunts and uncles and cousins there on that day, and we would *have the tree* (that is how we said it) before dinner. One of my aunts was head of the nursing division in Saskatchewan's public health department, and was a distinguished professional woman. I didn't know that about her then. What I knew was that each Christmas she came back home with an astounding assortment of rare and wonderful things from what I felt must be the centre of the great wide world, namely Regina. She used to bring us those packages of Swiss cheese, each tiny piece wrapped in silver paper, and decorations for the table (a Santa with reindeer and sleigh, pine-cone men painted iridescent white with red felt caps), and chocolate Santas in red and gold paper, and chocolate coins contained in heavy gold foil so that they looked like my idea of Spanish doubloons and pieces of eight, as in *Treasure Island*.

The dinner was enormous and exciting. We had *olives* to begin with. We rarely had olives at any other time, as they were expensive. My grandfather, of course, carved what was always known as The Bird, making the job into an impressive performance. He was never an eminently lovable man, but even he, with his stern ice-blue eyes, managed some degree of pleasantness at Christmas. The children at dinner were served last, which seems odd today. One of my memories is of myself at about six, sighing mightily as the plates were being passed to the adults and murmuring pathetically, "Couldn't I even have a crust?" My sense of drama was highly developed at a young age.

When the dishes were done—a mammoth task, washing all my grandmother's Limoges—we would make preparations to go home. I always had my own private foray into the kitchen then. I would go to the icebox (yes, icebox, with a block of ice delivered daily) and would tear off hunks of turkey, snatch a dozen or so olives, and wrap it all in wax paper. This was so I could have a small feast during the night, in case of sudden hunger, which invariably and improbably occurred each Christmas night.

The day of Christmas, however, began at home. The one I recall the best was the last Christmas we had with my father, for he died the next year. We were then living in my father's family home, a redbrick oddity with a rose window, a big dining room, a dozen nearly hidden cupboards and hidey-holes, and my father's study with the fireplace, above which hung a sinister bronze scimitar brought from India by an ancestor. I was nine that year, and my brother was two. The traditions in our family were strong. The children rose when they wakened (usually about 6 a.m. or earlier) and had their Christmas stockings. In those days, our stockings contained a Japanese orange at the toe, some red-and-white peppermint canes, a bunch of unshelled peanuts, and one or two small presents—a kaleidoscope or a puzzle consisting of two or three interlocked pieces of metal which you had to try to prise apart, and never could.

As my memory tells it to me, my very young brother and myself had our Christmas stockings in our parents' bedroom, and Christmas had officially begun. We were then sent back to bed until the decent hour of 7:30 or 8:00 a.m., at which time I could get dressed in my sweater and my plaid skirt with the straps over the shoulder, while my mother dressed my brother in his sweater and infant overalls. We then went down for breakfast. In our house, you always had breakfast before you had The Tree. This wasn't such a bad thing. Christmas breakfast was sausage rolls, which we never had for breakfast any other time. These had been made weeks before, and frozen in the unheated summer kitchen. We had frozen food years before it became commercially viable. I guess our only amazement about it when it came on the market was that they could do it in summer as well. After breakfast, we all went into the study, where we had to listen to the Empire Broadcast on the radio, a report from all those pink-coloured areas on the world map, culminating in the King's speech. The voices seemed to go on forever. I don't recall how my brother was kept pacified—with candy, probably—but I recall myself fidgeting. This was the ritual—the Empire Broadcast *before* The Tree, a practice which now seems to me to have been slightly bizarre, and yet probably was not so. Our parents wanted to hear it, and it those days it wasn't going to be repeated in capsule form on the late night news. I guess it also taught us that you could wait for what you wanted—but that's a concept about which I've always felt pretty ambiguous.

At last, at last, we could go into The Living Room for The Tree. The Living Room, I should say, was the only formal room in that house. We did not live in it; it was totally misnamed. It was For Best. It was the room in which my mother gave the afternoon teas which were then required of people like the wives of lawyers in towns like ours. The Living Room had a lot of stiff upholstered furniture, always just so. It was, as well, chilly. But it was the place for The Tree, and it seemed somehow the right place, something special.

And there it was, The Tree. *Oh.*

I could see now why we'd been so carefully kept out of the room until this moment. There, beside The Tree, were our presents. For my brother, a rocking horse, two horses cut out of wood and painted white with green flecks, joined by a seat between them. Our dad had made it, for he was a very good amateur carpenter. And for me—wow! A desk. A small desk, found in an attic, as I later learned, and painted by our dad, a bright blue with flower patterns, a desk which opened up and had your own private cubbyholes in it. My own desk. My first. That remains the nicest present that anyone ever gave me, the present from my parents when I was nine.

It was only many years later that I realized that the rocking-horse and the desk had been our presents then because no one could afford to buy anything much in that depression and drought year of 1935. And it wasn't until long afterwards, either, that I realized how lucky and relatively unscathed we'd been, and how many people in this country that year must have had virtually no Christmas at all.

One other aspect of my childhood Christmases was Lee Ling. He was the man who ran our town's Chinese restaurant, and he lived without his family for all the time he was there. In those days, Chinese wives were scarcely allowed into this country at all. My father did Lee's legal work, and every Christmas Lee gave us a turkey, a large box of chocolates, and a box of lichee nuts. You might say that Lee did it because he hoped to get on the right side of the lawyer. My father wasn't like that, and neither was Lee. The point of this story, however, is that Lee Ling continued at Christmas to give our family a turkey, a box of chocolates and a box of lichee nuts after my father died, for years, until Lee himself died. To me, that says something valuable about about Lee Ling and my father.

Much later on, when my own children were young and growing up, our Christmases became patterns which reflected my own Christmases many years ago, but with our own additions. We had ten Christmases in our house in England, Elm Cottage, before my children became adults and I moved back home to Canada to stay. Christmas in that house was always something very good and warm, and there were usually a lot of young Canadian visitors there with us at that time.

As in my childhood, the Christmas stockings were opened early in the morning. The difference was, with us, that my kids always made a Christmas stocking for me as well, their own idea. The stockings had candies, including the same kind of chocolate coins, but they also had a variety of joke presents, sometimes kids' books when my kids were no longer children, because we've always liked good children's books and we frequently give them to one another.

Some of the traditions continued. In our house, you always have breakfast before you have The Tree. But in our time, The Tree was in my study, not a "special" place, and we frequently went in wearing housecoats and dressing-gowns and bearing large mugs of coffee. The presents were distributed one at a time so everyone could look at each. We made it last about two hours. I don't think gifts need to be meaningless. I love opening presents from people who care about me, and I love giving presents to people I care about, hoping I've chosen something that fits their own personality, something that will be a symbol of my feeling for them.

Our dinner at Elm Cottage was always fairly hectic. I was in charge of what we called The Bird, as it had been called in my own childhood. I twittered and worried over that turkey, wondering if I had put it in the oven soon enough, or if I was going to overcook it to the point of total disaster. It always turned out fine, an amazing fact when one considers that our stove was so small as to be almost ridiculous and that even cramming a 15-pound turkey into it at all was a major task. The turkey, I modestly admit, was accompanied by some of the best sage-and-onion stuffing in the entire world. Our friend Alice always made her super cranberry sauce, which included walnuts and orange, and was the best I've ever tasted. Our friend Sandy always used to do the plum pudding, which she cleverly heated on a small electric burner set up in the hall, as there wasn't room on the stove. My daughter had been the one to organize the cake, a month before, and everyone had given it a stir for luck. It was a very co-operative meal. Yes, the women did prepare all the food. But the men carved The Bird, served the dinner, and did the dishes. It always seemed to me that our efforts meshed pretty well. Our friend Peter once said that Elm Cottage was a scene of "agreeable anarchy." I think it was, and that phrase certainly describes our Christmas dinners, at which we never had less than a dozen people, and sometimes more.

After dinner, we would move to The Music Room, which was our version of The Living Room, except that we really lived in it. It had a good stereo and a feeling that people could come in and sit around the fireplace and play their guitars and sing their own songs. This used to happen a lot, and always at Christmas. We made new traditions. One of my own favourites was a ritual which said that at some point in the evening, our friend Ian would play and sing two songs for me. Corny and out-of-date they may be, but I like them. They were "She Walks These Hills in a Long Black Veil" and "St. James Infirmary Blues."

Those Christmases at Elm Cottage had a feeling of real community. For me, this is what this festival is all about—the sense of God's grace, and the sense of our own family and extended family, the sense of human community.

Margaret Laurence's childhood home in Neepawa. This was her maternal grandfather's home, which is referred in the story as the "big brick house." She lived there after her father's death.

Ukrainian Christmas on the Homestead

Alice and David Didur
Near Garland, late 1930s to early 1940s

Alice Didur remembers a traditional Ukrainian Christmas on her parents' farm near Garland in the 1930s–40s. Many years later, her son David wrote down her memories for an article about Ukrainian Christmas in Manitoba, of which the following is an excerpt. The full article was published online at www.safekid.org. This passage is reprinted courtesy of David Didur.

There was a tiny community hall beside our one-room schoolhouse. On our last day of school before the Christmas holidays, we would have a Christmas party in the hall. We would decorate the hall, perform short skits and sing carols. Santa Claus would come, and he would hand out candies and other small treats to all of the children. I remember one special year, when my father was away from home working in the smelter in Coniston, Ontario. After distributing goodies, Santa sat down in a chair and called up Nestor Karpiak, my older brother! Santa gave him a Tinker Toy construction set.

Then Santa called up my sister Ann and me and handed each of us a beautiful porcelain doll. My mother said they were very dainty and fragile, and that we shouldn't play with them. She created a special place for them on the shelves of a corner cupboard, and there they sat on display. We had homemade dolls that were soft and pliable to play with, but we admired our two beautiful, fancy dolls. We didn't know it at the time, but our father had purchased the gifts for us with some of his earnings and had mailed them to our mom. She decided that Santa should give them to us as a reward for our hard work on the farm.

When the holidays started, we would go into the woods to find a Christmas tree. Normally, one pictures flat expanses of grassland when thinking of the prairies in Canada, but true prairies only occur in the southern parts of Alberta, Saskatchewan and Manitoba. The farm near Garland (in western Manitoba) was in the boreal coniferous forest, so there were pine and spruce trees in the forests suitable for traditional Christmas trees.

The tree was decorated with garlands made of silver tinsel, small glass ornaments, and clip-on candleholders into which three-inch (7.5 cm) red candles were inserted. The candles were lit for short periods of time in the evenings and were watched carefully to ensure the tree did not catch fire.

A couple of days before Christmas, children would go into the granary to get a few cups of wheat which would be placed into a strong bag, sprinkled with water, and then beaten with a stick for hours to loosen the husks from the grain. The husks would be rinsed away leaving the kernels of wheat and then boiled until the grains burst open. Wheat, water, honey and poppy seeds are the primary ingredients in making the special Christmas Eve dish—a sweet grain pudding called *kutia*. In prosperous times, chopped walnuts were added as well. Traditionally kutia is the first dish served at dinner and was rarely made during any other time of the year.

Ukrainian Christmas festivities start on Christmas Eve, which is on January 6th (as per the Gregorian calendar). The holy supper, *Sviata Vecherya*, is the focus of the day. My mother prepared twelve meatless dishes and father placed some hay on the table and covered it with a tablecloth—a reminder of the manger in Bethlehem. My father would then bring in a sheaf of wheat (called the *didukh*) and place it in a corner of the room. Part of the sheaf was spread out under the table, and my parents would hide nuts within it. We searched for the nuts after dinner was over. What a treat!

Braided bread, called a *kolach*, was placed in the centre of the table. When preparations were complete, my siblings and I eagerly watched for the first star in the eastern sky. When it was observed, dinner could begin!

Times were tough in the 1930s, so presents usually consisted of handmade articles of clothing and small treats which were opened on Christmas morning. January 7th was a family day and the following day was a time for friends stopping by. We referred to the day as a "feast of carolling." Friends and neighbours would sing together in a group and ask for donations, which were given to the church or to the poor.

I was one of twelve young people packed into a sleigh pulled by a pair of horses bundled up under blankets, singing in the cold crisp winter air as we glided along the snow-covered country roads. When we stopped at a farmhouse we were invited inside and offered freshly baked donuts that were served in a large bowl.

In many homes, older boys were taken aside and offered a shot of vodka—something to "warm up the insides." Carolling continued from noon until supper and then everyone would scatter to return to their homes.

January 19th, the Epiphany according to the Gregorian calendar, marked the end of holiday celebrations. Young children looked forward to this day very much. They would fill their pockets with wheat and walk down the roads to neighbouring farms. After knocking on the door and being greeted, they would recite a short verse and toss a small handful of wheat into the house. The children were usually rewarded with ten cents apiece and wishes were exchanged for a happy and prosperous season in the new year.

Happenings From Our Farm

Marcel Pitre
Lac du Bonnet, 1930s–40s

Sleigh rides feature prominently in many of the stories in this anthology, and Marcel Pitre's story is no exception. He paints a beautiful picture of Christmas in Lac du Bonnet in the 1930s and '40s.

CAN YOU RECALL, FROM the youngster deep within you, that wonderful Christmas season of snow, crisp air, and winter clothing combined with secret thoughts of giving and receiving? The rush of the season probably caused most of us to muse with anticipation of what was to come, especially as children. Sleep never failed to continue our daylight thoughts as we dreamt through the night. On the farm, discussing coming events with a friend a half mile away was difficult. Consequently, dreaming—of the daytime variety—consumed a large part of idle moments that we were sometimes afforded. Christmas time and the Christmas tree and all that it suggested was solid in our young minds.

A much looked-forward-to tradition in our family, and many others, was the horse and sleigh ride to Midnight Mass at our village church in Lac du Bonnet. It was right up there with Christmas dreams, all the better if cousins of our age were visiting for a sleepover. And this event was always well planned! Our big all-purpose grain box was installed on the horse sleigh with its floor generously covered with sweet-smelling hay, while the horse harnesses were elegantly decorated with sparse plumes and the few short rows of bells that we owned.

The ride to town and the visiting was as great an enticement as the service inside of the church. It was a time for neighbours and those from some distance to get together both before and after the service. It was a time to chat of the summer and fall farm happenings and to break bread together in a lesser manner an hour or so after midnight if the weather cooperated, and it always did in some fashion.

Notre-Dame-du-Lac Church

The trip to town and back was the highlight of the evening for everyone. The idea was to get there early. We were always fresh and ready to go. Older brothers and sisters were home for the holidays, and invited friends made the occasion even greater. Mother and Dad occupied the preferential seats in the all-purpose box while we picked our druthers, though most did not sit still. Homemade sleds and old toboggans were hitched to the back of the sleigh, sometimes in tandem. There were many spills and just as many stops for catch-up duty for the fallen-behind sledders. Faithful Brownie, our always eager and enthusiastic dog, did not have to be harnessed to a sled, which gave him ample time to enjoy the entire journey, barking at anything and everything. He more than doubled the distance to town in one outing. Needless to say there were slotted moments to brush off snow or debris from hay-wrestling before entering the church.

After Mass, featuring Christmas hymns and happy thoughts, Merry Christmas exchanges consumed some time. It was not unheard of that, during this occasion, the younger adults and some of those not so young would visit the local after-closing-time-watering-hole which conveniently existed just across the street. It had a darkened backdoor entrance which featured "cheery anti-freeze" inside ... considered necessary for our return journey.

The much-quicker ride home led to homemade music, singing and a homemade meal. Given all the confusion and enjoyment the Christmas celebrations provided, the after-Mass meal usually turned into a late breakfast. But that was not unusual as breakfast could be at anytime. Presents were always exchanged after the meal when all were sufficiently satisfied and a bit calmed down.

One of the central forms of sustenance which always adorned the table Christmas mornings was Mother's pâté. This ecstasy consisted of a mixture of rabbit and pork combined with the world's best spices, cooked in a frying pan. It was then baked in a thick coating of extra special dough with slashed openings on its surface, and always cooked to perfection. The fragrance added so much to its appearance and it indeed was a tawny delight to behold ... and a mealtime treat to eat. "Pâté by Mother" was well known by family, relatives, and friends. That part of our Christmas nighttime get-together was another welcome and *filling* highlight.

You have now been served a serving of our after-dark Christmas experience from the usual Yuletide happenings from our farm, 13–15–10E, 1 & 1/2 miles northeast, as the crow flies, of Lac du Bonnet, Manitoba, c. 1930s to the mid- and even late '40s.

The King's Speech, Christmas 1939

King George VI
December 25, 1939

A tradition for many Manitoban families was to listen to the royal message on Christmas morning. In 1939, with the world about to be embroiled in another war, families around the Commonwealth listened intently to King George VI's reassuring words. He ended the nine minute broadcast with a verse from the poem, "God Knows" by Minnie Louise Haskins.

HE FESTIVAL WHICH WE know as Christmas is above all the festival of peace and of the home. Among all free peoples the love of peace is profound, for this alone gives security to the home.

But true peace is in the hearts of men and it is the tragedy of this time that there are powerful countries whose whole direction and policy are based on aggression and the suppression of all that we hold dear for mankind. It is this that has stirred our peoples and given them a unity unknown in any previous war. We feel in our hearts that we are fighting against wickedness, and this conviction will give us strength from day to day to persevere until victory is assured.

At home we are, as it were, taking the strain for what may lie ahead of us, resolved and confident. We look with pride and thankfulness on the never-failing courage and devotion of the Royal Navy, upon which, throughout the last four months, has burst the storm of ruthless and unceasing war.

And when I speak of our Navy today, I mean all the men of our Empire who go down to the sea in ships, the Mercantile Marine, the mine-sweepers, the trawlers and drifters, from the senior officers to the last boy who has joined up.

To every one in this great Fleet I send a message of gratitude and greeting, from myself as from all my peoples. The same message I send to the gallant Air Force which, in co-operation with the Navy, is our sure shield of defence. They are daily adding laurels to those that their fathers won.

I would send a special word of greeting to the Armies of the Empire, to those who have come from afar, and in particular to the British Expeditionary Force.

Their task is hard. They are waiting, and waiting is a trial of nerve and discipline. But I know that when the moment comes for action they will prove themselves worthy of the highest traditions of their great Service.

And to all who are preparing themselves to serve their country, on sea or land or in the air, I send my greeting at this time. The men and women of our far-flung Empire working in their several vocations, with the one same purpose, all are members of the great Family of Nations which is prepared to sacrifice everything that freedom of spirit may be saved to the world.

Such is the spirit of the Empire; of the great Dominions, of India, of every Colony, large or small. From all alike have come offers of help, for which the mother country can never be sufficiently grateful. Such unity in aim and in effort has never been seen in the world before. I believe from my heart that the cause which binds together my peoples and our gallant and faithful Allies is the cause of Christian civilisation. On no other basis can a true civilisation be built. Let us remember this through the dark times ahead of us and when we are making the peace for which all men pray.

A new year is at hand. We cannot tell what it will bring. If it brings peace, how thankful we shall all be. If it brings us continued struggle we shall remain undaunted.

In the meantime I feel that we may all find a message of encouragement in the lines which, in my closing words, I would like to say to you:

"I said to the man who stood at the Gate of the Year, 'Give me a light that I may tread safely into the unknown.' And he replied, 'Go out into the darkness, and put your hand into the Hand of God. That shall be to you better than light, and safer than a known way.'"

May that Almighty Hand guide and uphold us all.

American servicemen visiting Winnipeg, Christmas 1942. From left to right: Bill Johnson, John Andrews, and Raymond Buggert. The soldiers, from the 111th Ordnance Company, were in Manitoba for cold weather training at Camp Shiloh. Photo credit: Andrea Sutcliffe.

Top left: Margaret Owen's father, Lt. Frederick Victor Dennis, in 1941. Top right: Margaret's parents, Lucy and Victor Dennis, on his departure from Winnipeg. Bottom: Margaret (right) with mother and siblings, Roger and Barbara, in 1942. Photo credit: Margaret Dennis Owen.

The Home Front

Margaret Dennis Owen
Winnipeg, 1941

Christmas, 1941 was a stressful time for many Manitobans. Soldiers with the Winnipeg Grenadiers were involved in the defence of Hong Kong, which ultimately fell on Christmas Day. Many soldiers were killed, wounded, or captured by Japanese forces. Families back in Manitoba waited for news of their loved ones while trying to go about their normal lives and prepare for the holidays. Margaret Dennis Owen was just a child when her father went to war, but she recalls clearly and poignantly those anxious days.

DURING THE DAYS BEFORE Christmas, Mother followed her annual tradition of baking Scotch oatcakes and shortbread; her special gift to her sister Henrietta, and her two brothers, Charlie and Billy, and their families. Uncle Billy's wife Maude was so crippled by rheumatoid arthritis that she was unable to bake, and Uncle Charlie's wife Agnes was bedridden as the result of a stroke.

Mother also put up the Christmas tree, bought gifts, and played Christmas carols on the piano. She wanted to make Christmas bright and happy for all of us, but it was a time of great anxiety. She listened regularly to the CBC radio newscasts first thing in the morning, again at noon and suppertime, and late in the evening. The radio so dominated our lives that one day Barbara announced, "When this war's over, I'm never going to listen to the news again!"

For almost three weeks the Canadian troops in Hong Kong fought a losing battle against insurmountable odds. Although our men fought valiantly, there were only 14,000 of them, and they were under-trained. They were certainly no match for the 60,000-strong Japanese army that had become battle-hardened during ten years of fighting against China. After three weeks of combat, lacking food, water and ammunition, the Canadians had nothing left to give, and they were finally forced to surrender on Christmas Day. On Boxing Day the *Free Press* and the *Tribune* proclaimed the news.

The Grenadiers, in spite of their defeat, were proclaimed heroes. "The news that fighting has ceased in Hong Kong marks the end of one of the most gallant episodes in the history of Canadian arms," said Defence Minister J. L. Ralston.

Lieutenant-Colonel J. N. Siemens, commander of the second battalion of the Grenadiers, paid tribute to the men of the first battalion with these words: "While we deeply regret the inevitable loss that is sure to follow in the wake of the surrender of Hong Kong, we are justly proud of the gallant stand made by the men of the Winnipeg Grenadiers and their sister regiment from Quebec. They have added a glorious page to the annals of Canadian heroism."

And from the elderly Lieutenant-Colonel J. B. Mitchell, who had commanded the regiment until his retirement in 1920, came these words: "I always knew that the Winnipeg Grenadiers had the stamina of good old Anglo-Saxon stock to hold out in the face of great difficulty."

The families of the Grenadiers wanted only to receive word of the men's safety, but the *Free Press* warned that it might take weeks to obtain casualty lists through the International Red Cross. Although Mother didn't hear directly from Daddy, she faithfully wrote regular letters, telling him all the family news. Her first letter after the fall of Hong Kong was full of details about our first Christmas without him. Before he left he had given her money to buy gifts.

> *My Dearest One,*
>
> *I hardly know what to say to you after this terrible time of trial and suspense, but I want you to know that God will bring you back to us one day. I ask nothing more of this life than to have you home again to help raise this lovely family with me. I know only too well what you must have felt, and I have prayed constantly that you be given strength and courage and patience to live through the days until we meet again.*
>
> *I tried to make Christmas as bright as possible for the children, and our friends were all so kind to us. We had several invitations to dinner. I would have to see you to tell you all the lovely things people did to help us.*
>
> *Your present to me was a lovely gold-filled locket and chain, and I wear it with your picture in it. The picture is one of you smiling at me in a canoe on the river, and I put one of myself in the other side. I wear it always, dear, even in bed. I only take it off when I wash myself. If I am wearing a dress that doesn't suit it, I just slip it inside. It is my lucky charm. Roger is so cute—he is always wanting to open my locket, and he kisses our pictures, saying "I love you, Daddy. I love you, Mummy." I didn't tell him to do it, either! I gave the girls beautiful dolls, and Roger a big delivery truck from Daddy. Honestly, dear, they talk of you constantly, and when Roger can't do exactly as he pleases, he says "My Daddy told me to!" He is always kissing your picture and telling everybody about you. Barbara's prayers for you are most touching, and Margaret's too.*

When Daddy received this letter, he wrote back, sounding sad and lonely.

> *Lucy Darling,*
>
> *Have just received your letter and it's lovely to get news of so many friends, but especially of yourself and our three dear children.*
>
> *Am still keeping fit and am studying bridge to help pass the time.*

The Home Front

Your letter made me quite homesick and longing for the time when we can be reunited. I'm very glad everyone is so kind to you. It relieves my anxiety considerably. I DO wish I could see you all again. Please God it won't be long.

Look after the children and yourself for me.

Ever your loving
Vic
(F. V. Dennis)

On the home front, the people of Winnipeg celebrated the Christmas season as usual, visiting friends, going to parties, skating and tobogganing. On New Year's Eve, the Capitol and Metropolitan Theatres ran double features, the Puffin Ski Club held a ball in the Royal Alexandra Hotel, and many people held private parties. Mother had been invited out to dinner, but decided to stay home with us instead. She lit the fireplace, and we played Snakes and Ladders, and checkers, and drank hot cocoa with marshmallows on top before being tucked into bed well before midnight.

I didn't feel like sleeping. I knelt on my bed and leaned my elbows on the windowsill, pressing my forehead against the frosty glass and gazing down on the quiet, snow-covered street. Lights shone from the neighbouring houses, and smoke from the chimneys curled into the wintry sky. My new Christmas pyjamas, pink flannelette covered with playful white kittens, hugged my little girl's body as I remembered the Christmas just past. Even without Daddy, it had been a happy time.

There were parties to go to, both before and after Christmas. Mr. Brown next door belonged to the Kiwanis Club, and he took the three of us, along with his two children, Douglas and Valerie, to the annual Kinsmen's Club Children's Christmas party in the elegant red and gold ballroom on the top floor of the Marlborough Hotel downtown. The room had been decorated for Christmas with a huge tree, tinsel hung from the chandeliers and big red bows adorned the walls. We ate hot dogs and ice cream and cookies and chocolate milk. Santa Claus appeared on the balcony above the ballroom in his red suit and white-bearded chubbiness, jingling his bells and waving to us before descending to the stage where he doled out gifts to every child, along with bags of those shiny, hard, tongue-burning Christmas candies.

During the season many people came to our house to visit, bringing flowers and bottles of sherry for Mother, and candy canes and Christmas oranges for us. Faces ruddy and noses dripping from the cold, guests struggled to open the heavy storm door, letting gusts of frigid air into the front hall. Once inside, they'd remove their snowy boots, stamping and laughing, and then carry their fresh-smelling fur coats and hats up to Mother's bedroom where they'd lay them across her bed. They'd blow their noses into freshly ironed linen handkerchiefs and run their fingers through their hat-mussed hair. We children would follow them every step of the way, giggling and chattering. Mother would make tea, and bring out oatcakes and cheese and shortbread and fruitcake, and we'd get to stay up late. After everyone had gone home, Mother would turn off all the lights in the living room except the ones on the Christmas tree. We had a special string of Mickey Mouse lights. Every bulb had a little glass shade with a picture of Mickey or Minnie Mouse, Pluto, Goofy or Donald or Daisy Duck. We'd sit in the soft glow, singing carols. I loved it when we sang "Silent Night." I'd imagine snow gently falling around the manger where the baby Jesus lay sleeping, and angels singing in the bright sky overhead.

Now it was all over. Mother would take down the Christmas tree and put away all the decorations, and I'd go back to school. A train whistled hauntingly in the distance, its mournful sound piercing the frosty darkness. It seemed to be crying for Daddy and for all the other soldiers and sailors and airmen who were so far away from home. I thought about the train that took us to meet Daddy in Brockville, and the other train that took him away to war. I wondered what he was doing at that very moment. Did he have turkey for Christmas dinner? Did he get any candy? We'd sent him a parcel with his favourite black and green jellybeans in it, and some cigarettes and warm socks. I gave him an Agatha Christie book, Barbara a deck of cards and Roger a cribbage board. Did he get the things in time for Christmas? My lips moved in silent prayer, my breath making a small circle of mist on the cold windowpane.

"God, please take care of Daddy. Keep him safe and end the war soon so that he can come home again." Then I snuggled under the covers and closed my eyes. I could hear the muffled sounds coming from the RCA Victor console radio in the living room as Mother listened to the war-torn world welcoming in the year 1942.

Christmas Wish

Evelyn Ballantyne
Opaskwayak Cree Nation, 1940s

Growing up on the Opaskwayak Cree Nation, Evelyn Ballantyne remembers a special Christmas. It was to be her last one before she and her sister were sent to residential school.

HE WOOD STOVE STOOD at the centre of the room, giving warmth to those who sat around exchanging legends and stories of days gone by. The aroma of fresh baked bannock filled the house.

Our home was a two-storey structure. Houses in the reservation I grew up in were similar in design. The main floor was an open area, where the ordinary everyday activities took place. The upstairs served as a sleeping area and beds were arranged in such a way that girls slept in one corner, parents in one, and boys slept in another corner of the room. The chimney provided warmth to the upstairs.

What I remember most about those days, was the excitement that could be felt for days. The celebration of Christmas played such an important part in our family and community life, and represented a time of great enjoyment.

It was a time for feasts and visitors. It seemed that it was never-ending. The sharing of food and good times was to be seen all over the community. I remember my mother and father taking my sister and I along as they made their visits. The neighbours we visited would make sure that treats for children were abundant. My sister and I would sit on the floor by our parents and listen as they told stories about hunting, fishing, and trapping. Every now and then, everyone would burst out laughing. Such a joyous time. I can close my eyes and think to when I was a child and it seems like it was only yesterday.

The first week of the two-week celebration was set aside for visiting and cooking tons and tons of food. By Christmas Eve, the excitement was unbearable for us. We were told to be in bed earlier than usual as Santa would pass by our house if we stayed up late. Believing so strongly in Santa, we of course obeyed, and were on our best behaviour.

This particular Christmas, the house looked wonderful with its glittering decorations. There was no electricity at the time, and that made everything in our house even more warm. As my sister and I climbed the stairs to our bed, we took one last look at the beautiful tree. We whispered into the night wondering what we would find under the tree the next morning.

It wasn't long before we heard the steps of our mother making her way upstairs. She always made sure we said our evening prayers, and this night was no exception. As she left, she lowered the brightness of the coal oil lamp that was beside our bed. Now there was only a faint light in the room.

The next morning, Christmas Day! I woke up my sister and within minutes we were running down the stairs. We stopped and looked under the tree. All the presents, so carefully wrapped, looked beautiful. In no time we were on the floor by the tree, looking at the tags with our names on the packages. The sounds of our excitement woke our parents. As usual, we received what we had wished for. I had dropped many hints to my mother about the black doll I had wanted so badly. To this day, I don't know why the doll had to be black. Regardless, my Christmas wish had come true. In one of the packages I unwrapped, there was my little black baby doll.

The rest of the day was spent going to church, eating our Christmas dinner, visiting other neighbours, eating, eating and eating at different feasts throughout the community. I have never forgotten that day and it will always hold a very special place in my memories. Later, I was to find out why the doll was so important to me.

The next three years would not be the same, for my sister and I were sent to a residential school. That doll represented stability, security, and a reminder of my family back home. My sister and I were lucky in that our parents made sure there was enough money to pay for our train fare for us to be home for Christmas. I'll never forget that.

Today, I have carried on the traditions I was taught by my parents. At Christmas, while some values and customs may have changed, we still celebrate by sharing the Christmas dinner and the exchanging of gifts. Within our own family we still go house to house for feasts . . . but that long ago Christmas will always be memorable.

Christmas at Our House

Gordon Billings
Near MacGregor, late 1940s

Gordon Billings grew up on a farm near MacGregor and attended Southend School, a one-room schoolhouse. When young Gordon left school every day, it followed him home—not because he had homework, but because his teacher lived with Gordon's family on the farm!

WELL, LET'S SET THE stage: I lived on a farm south of MacGregor, and I spent the first nine years of my school life in a one-room school. It was the same school that my mother and father attended when they first came to Manitoba from Ontario about 1900. (Their families were not known to each other then.)

The student population was about 23 to 25 (grades 1 to 8, plus the teacher had to supervise the grades 9s who took the grade by correspondence). She was expected to teach each grade in the one-room school.

The school was less than 3/4 of a mile from our house, so the teacher stayed with us. As a result, during the school year I never got away from the teacher (seven days a week)!

The school was heated by a wood furnace. The trustees acquired many cords of wood over the winter, which they sawed into furnace-length in the spring and let it dry over the summer. When the snow came we were reduced to sleigh and horse as the roads were not plowed and there was lots of snow.

Anyway, each year the school put on a concert just before Christmas. The class would practise the concert for a few weeks before the big evening. The men would set the stage at the back of the school; we would attend school during the day and return with our parents at about seven o'clock. We all came by horse and sleigh and put the horses in the school barn. Those horses that did not fit in the barn were covered in horse blankets and left outside.

I can remember hearing the hissing of the Coleman lamp hanging from the ceiling with a shade on it so the light would shine on the stage. All the school kids had a part in the concert—some would do a play, others would recite a Christmas poem and all of us would sing in a Christmas choir. The concert was the signal of the Christmas holidays and CHRISTMAS at our house.

With the windup of the Christmas concert, it was holidays for about two weeks. The teacher was gone and I could live like a kid again!

Manitoba at Christmas

Now, when I got up on Christmas morning, I could open my stocking and discover what Santa had brought, which normally was something small. I hoped the big gift was under the tree! But we had to wait until the afternoon, after dinner, to open those gifts.

The special roaster (a chicken or turkey) was readied for the oven (a wood stove), and took all morning to prepare. We got out the good dishes and my mother got out the goodies that she had baked. We always had my two sisters, Uncle Fred (a bachelor) and Grandma Acheson (my mother's mother) and occasionally the Browns (Mr. and Mrs. Brown (my mother's sister) and their daughter Louise, who was about my age).

We finished up the big dinner and at last we could open the presents under the tree. Somehow my mother kept them hidden from us, even though looking back they were likely from the Eaton's catalogue.

The men did the farm chores and sat around and told stories about the past year or years gone by, while the women folk were in the kitchen doing dishes and we kids played with our gifts and went outside to play in the yard or in the straw stack. To play in the stack was a big deal because we needed all the straw for bedding for the animals over the winter, but on Christmas Day my father allowed us to play in it.

With all the excitement of the day we kids were tired and while we tried to stay up late, our eyes became heavy with sleep and we soon went to bed.

Boys and girls at Southend School. Gordon Billings is second from the right in the top photo. Photo credit: Gordon Billings.

Sheet music for "Good King Wenceslas."

Who Are The Saints?

Mary Louise Chown
Winnipeg, 1953

The Christmas carol "Good King Wenceslas" often comes to mind when I'm stepping through deep snow. I'm reminded of how the king forged a path in the snow for his weary page to follow. For storyteller Mary Louise Chown, the good king's name evokes a poignant memory from childhood, which was sparked by a dinner conversation with a friend.

> "Good King Wenceslas looked out, on the feast of Stephen;
> When the snow lay round about, deep and crisp and even."

WENCESLAS. IT IS VERY strange and mysterious how one word can call up a thousand images ... a whole story. My friend Grace came over for supper one night last October and she told me about her stay in Prague, the beautiful old medieval city, full of music. Then she saw the castle of King Wenceslas, built on a high cliff overlooking the river Vltava.

I have not told Grace this, but as soon as she mentioned Wenceslas I was eight years old again, trudging through the snow that lay "deep and crisp and even," my head bent down against the bitter north wind that drove itself down Claremont Avenue. There was no snow blanketing the Winnipeg world as Grace and I sat and talked over supper, yet in the space of a second, a winter scene was unfolding itself from the recesses of my memory.

December 1953. I was eight years old. Dad had died in November of that year and my mother, my brother and I were on our way to the movies for the second time that week. We were Catholic and my favourite part of Christmas every year was always Advent ... the getting ready ... pulling out the Christmas records, playing the carols and the hymns, practising them for the school Christmas concert where Father Empson always sat large and encouraging in the front row.

But the winter of 1953 was different. After Dad died we went out a lot, and we always walked. Looking back now, I wonder if we didn't have a car until my mother found work. In Norwood at that time, there were two movie theatres across the park at the end of our street, and two drugstores with lunch counters where you could buy milkshakes and sodas.

My brother and I didn't question why we had to go out to the movies two or three times a week that winter. What normal eight or ten year old would? It was a dream come true! I remember the cold north wind blowing on our faces as we walked along Claremont Street to Coronation Park. Then across the park to Tache and Marion where the shows were. I remember walking beside my mother and crying because the wind cut into my face. She didn't chide me. She simply said, "Walk in my footsteps. I'll break the wind for you."

Mom wore a thick, velvety black beaver coat and those black boots with fur at the top which came just above the ankle and tied in front. She strode along the snowy sidewalk like a large black bear. I walked along behind and the wind no longer bit into my face and cheeks.

> "In his master's steps he trod, where the snow lay dinted;
> Heat was in the very sod which the saint had printed."

Well who are the saints anyway? I had been taught at school that they started out as ordinary people who did something brave or kind. Wasn't my mother both of these things? Brave to keep on living as normally as possible, keeping us cheerful and hopeful. Kind to take us to the show so often each week, feeding us along the way with milkshakes and sandwiches.

This was my song. It didn't matter that there was no poor peasant to whom we were bringing food. I was that page, trudging through snow that was "deep and crisp and even." The sandwiches my mother carried and the milkshake we stopped for was to feed us … poor starving trio without our dad. It didn't matter that we were walking so purposefully not towards home, but away to the cold comfort of a movie house.

Who was King Wenceslas? This is less clear. Perhaps Mom and Dad were both Wenceslas. Dad was the Wenceslas at the beginning, when he looks out of his castle window and sees someone walking through the bitter snow. After all, I had been assured that my father was in fact in Heaven and could have chosen this very moment to look down on us as we worked our way north on Claremont Avenue. Then the scene shifts with the ease only possible in the mind's eye. My face is stinging with cold and now Wenceslas is walking ahead of me, shielding me from the bitter weather with her own body. The carol began its part in shaping the story of who I am even while I walked along on those far off winter nights and it continues to bring into sharp and instant focus that feeling of being at once without, and yet protected.

Going to the Big City: Shopping at Eaton's

Wayne Chan

For many Manitobans, urban and rural alike, Eaton's department store in downtown Winnipeg was *the* place to go for Christmas shopping. Whether it was making a special trip to the city for the holidays or ordering from the Eaton's catalogue—which was a lifeline for goods and supplies for Manitoban communities—the store epitomized the holidays.

Letters to Santa

In the days before Canada Post replied to letters to Santa, the postal service delivered the correspondence to Eaton's, where the letters received personalized replies written by the store's staff. In addition to mail, letters could be dropped in Santa's Mailbox at Toyland, and they were also collected from children during the Santa Claus parade.

Eaton's Displays

New York had Macy's and Cleveland had HigBee's, but the Eaton's store in Winnipeg could rival them all for its elaborate Christmas displays. Children, with their parents in tow, flocked to its windows during the Yuletide season, eager to see the magical exhibits depicting nursery rhymes or fairytales. The moving papier-mâché figures seen in the 1950s and '60s were built by veterans and craftsmen after World War II and were powered by war surplus motors. The windows facing Portage Avenue featured a changing theme every year, while the window at Portage and Hargrave St. was reserved for a nativity scene; in later decades this was changed to a family Christmas scene. In the late 1960s or early '70s, Eaton's acquired some mechanically animated storybook vignettes from Dayton's department store in Minneapolis, which were integrated into the window displays. They later became part of "Santa's Village" on the seventh floor of the store. When Eaton's closed in 1999, the vignettes were transferred to the Manitoba Children's Museum, where they can now be seen.

Continued on next page →

Eaton's display window in downtown Winnipeg, ca. 1945. Animals in other windows held letters which together spelled "Toyland."

Eaton's Santa Claus Parade

The first Eaton's Santa Claus parade in Winnipeg was held in 1905, the same year the downtown store opened. The parade began as a modest affair, with just Santa's sleigh drawn by four horses in the first year, but by the 1920s, the parade had eight floats, along with a number of automobiles that were decorated for the parade. The number of spectators continued to grow as well. By the late 1940s, there were estimated to be as many as 75,000 people attending the event. Eaton's stopped hosting the parade after 1966 due to rising costs, and it was turned over to the Winnipeg Firefighters' Club for the next ten years, until The Winnipeg Jaycees took over its organization. The parade is currently sponsored by Manitoba Hydro.

Going to the Big City: Shopping at Eaton's

Santa float in Eaton's Santa parade in Winnipeg, 1949.

In the early years of the parade, the procession began at the CPR train station and made its way to the store. Eaton's came up with creative reasons to explain Santa's arrival in Winnipeg by train, rather than by sleigh. In 1905, the store claimed to have received a telegram from Santa shortly before he was expected to arrive, in which he said that his reindeer had drowned! "While crossing a bay the ice gave way and my deer and myself were precipitated into the freezing cold water. I was warmly clad and did not much mind. The deer, however, were less fortunate; they managed to gain solid ground, but they were so badly chilled that both died a few hours afterwards. I have made arrangements to have them properly buried ... The deer gone, I pressed into service a train of splendid huskies and they are bringing me to the nearest railway station. I can make it easily and I will be in Winnipeg Saturday morning, sure."

Continued on next page →

In 1906, Santa's reindeer failed him again by not travelling fast enough, and he was forced to charter a train. The year after, his reindeer became too tired on the way to Winnipeg and Eaton's had to send out two cars to pick him up—one car for Santa and one for his "four bears." In 1908, they seemed to have forgone any parade and simply decided to "magically transport" Santa and his North Pole home to Eaton's Toyland. Santa dispensed with those unreliable reindeer in 1909 and arrived on horseback, travelling with six "Esquimaux," as proof that he came from the North Pole. In 1910, Eaton's decided to drop the pretense altogether and had Santa arrive by train without any further explanation, and in the following year, they didn't even bother explaining how he would arrive, but merely that he would be at Eaton's Toyland on a particular Saturday morning.

Eaton's Beauty Dolls

A prized gift for many little girls was the Eaton's Beauty Doll, which were a series of dolls originally made in Germany, with bisque heads, fully jointed composition bodies, and glass sleeping eyes. A new doll was released by Eaton's every year in its Fall and Winter catalogue. A trademark feature of the doll was a red ribbon across its chest, with gold lettering identifying it as an "Eaton's Beauty." The dolls were introduced by Eaton's in 1900 and quickly became a bestseller. They were originally produced by Armand Marseille in Germany, but during the two world wars the dolls were made in Canada—by the Dominion Toy Manufacturing Company in World War I, and by the Reliable Toy Company in World War II.

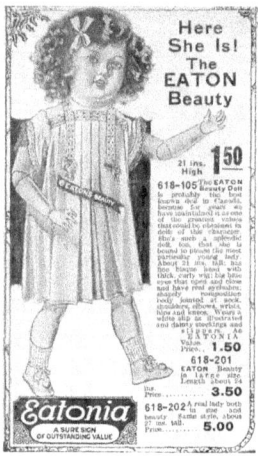

Eaton's Beauty Doll, 1925.

Punkinhead

Based on the success of Rudolph the Red-Nosed Reindeer, which was created by U. S. retailer Montgomery Ward in 1939, Eaton's decided to come up with its own Christmas character in the form of a bear named Punkinhead, because of his woolly tuft of orange hair. Punkinhead was created and drawn by Winnipeg animator Charles Thorson, who had worked for Walt Disney and Warner Brothers and is credited with creating and naming Bugs Bunny. Much like

Rudolph, Punkinhead was a social outcast—not for his nose, but for his unruly hair. Punkinhead's back-story was described in *Punkinhead: The Sad Little Bear*, which was published in 1948. According to the tale, Santa Claus visited Bear-Land one year on his way to Eaton's Toyland and treated everyone to honey sodas. One clown became ill after drinking too much soda and could not participate in the parade. All the bears wanted to be the one to replace him, but none could fit the clown's hat, which was too large. They quickly realized that little Punkinhead, with his thick mop of hair, was the only one who could wear the hat, and he became Santa's helper in the parade.

Punkinhead became an instant success, and a series of children's books and radio programs, and all manner of Punkinhead merchandise, soon followed. There were Punkinhead bowls and mugs, watches, mittens and toques, and he even had a theme song.

Once upon a time, not so very long ago, there was a big, leafy, green forest where families and families of bears lived. Because so many bears lived there, it was known far and wide as Bear-Land. A finer lot of bears you never did see! All brown and woolly and cuddly. All happy and scampery. All, that is, except one. And he was very sad.

He was sad because he didn't look like the other little bears at all. He was brown

Punkinhead, the Sad Little Bear.

Crowds at Hargrave St. and Graham Ave. in Winnipeg waiting for the arrival of Santa at the end of the Eaton's parade in 1934.

A Tale of Christmas Past at Eaton's

Judy Gerstel
Winnipeg, early 1950s

Toronto writer and journalist Judy Gerstel grew up in Winnipeg. She reminisces about simpler times, when the big excitement at Christmas was heading to Eaton's magical Toyland. Her story was previously published on EverythingZoomer.com is reprinted courtesy of Judy Gerstel and ZoomerMedia Limited.

ONCE UPON A TIME, kiddies, there was Toyland.
No, not an app.
Not toyland.com.

There was Toyland at Eaton's.

It was a time long ago when there were no apps, no smartphones and no iPads.

Your grandmother was a little girl, and Eaton's Toyland was on the fifth floor of a department store that you could walk through, not scroll through.

You reached the promised land by taking an escalator or an elevator with an operator wearing white gloves.

And when you arrived in that enchanted place, everything you always wanted was displayed there, all at the same time in the same place—not one screen at a time—amid glitter and ribbons and snowflakes and helper elves.

What wasn't there were Disney princess dolls (not even Elsa!) or walking dinosaurs or flying fairies or kid-sized cars with batteries.

There were games like checkers and Monopoly that came in a box with a board and pieces you could hold in your hand and move around the board.

Because these could be easily lost after the game was opened—that meant unwrapping the package and taking the cover off the box, not touching an icon—your father gave you a purple velvet Crown Royal bag with gold strings that could be pulled tight to keep the pieces safe.

There were Meccano sets and Lincoln logs and Plasticine and books like *The Hardy Boys* and *Treasure Island* and *Nancy Drew* and *Little Women*. There were electric trains and cars and trucks with no remote controls and dolls and dollhouses and doll prams.

There were no character dolls from movies or TV shows. but you might find a nurse doll or a ballerina doll or even your heart's desire—a Barbara Ann Scott doll.

And there, through an arch of candy canes and evergreen boughs, reigning over Toyland, was Santa Claus.

And even if you were a little girl who'd shed her snow pants in the store and wore a short dress with bare thighs, you got to sit on Santa's lap, and nobody thought anything but how sweet it was as you told Santa that what you really wanted most was a talking doll because you were shy and that's what all the girls said, and he smiled and sent you back to your mother with a candy cane.

After Toyland, there were still more treats at Eaton's in the Grill Room where the waitress gave you a menu that was a mask shaped like the head of a teddy bear called Punkinhead. And then, before you went home, you stopped at the Hostess Shop, where ladies in uniform with handkerchiefs tucked in their pockets carefully put Red Velvet cakes and chicken pot pies in folded boxes, and you got two gingerbread men, one for now and one for later.

And now, kiddies, it's time to go sleep and tomorrow we'll go to toysrus.ca and indigo.ca and target.ca and walmart.ca and amazon.ca, and you can show me all the presents you want to put on your list.

Barbara Ann Scott doll. Image courtesy of the Red Deer Museum and Art Gallery.

Memories of the Last Day Before Christmas

Grace Warkentin
Steinbach, early 1950s

Grace Warkentin grew up in Steinbach, in a large family of nine girls and two boys. She recalls a special Christmas when she was around ten years old. Her story was first published in the Mennonite Mirror *in 1980 and is reprinted with permission.*

AT 506 MAIN STREET in Steinbach, Christmas was not that much different than in any other household. But now that I am grown, these memories are special and I will share a rather disjointed collection of them with you.

I was about 10 years old that year. Some people began Christmas preparations early in December. But not us! When the 24th day of December rolled around, that was our cue. The girls (nine of us) usually decided that we should have a tree, and then my brother Peter was elected to go and pick one out. And woe be to him if it was less than perfect.

While Peter was selecting the tree from those remaining behind Pete Vogt's store, we got out the boxes of decorations and began sprucing (literally) up our rooms. This always got us in the spirit of the day. Sometimes we were so spirited that Mom had to yell at us to cease from such spirited activity.

Grace Warkentin

Next important of course was all the melting snow for the numerous manes of hair to be washed. Then the bath water had to be pumped and heated. We had without question the tastiest pump water you ever swallowed. And we weren't the only ones who thought so. Most of our neighbours were of the same opinion. I used to see how many pumps of the handle were necessary before the first water came. Five swift strokes was the best I could ever do, but every time I pumped I had the chance to beat that record.

Today, as I was pumping, wintry sounds filled the air. The familiar twang of a chainsaw came from the direction of Nightengales, behind us. The jingling of sleigh bells on a caboose going to East Steinbach. (No power toboggans yet.) Then, faintly, but distinctly, I heard yet another familiar sound. Someone was whistling. Not "Noël" or even *"Leise rieselt der Schnee."* No. I knew immediately who it was, because it is the only song I ever heard him whistle. "School days, school days, O' those golden rule days." The bachelor from across the street was coming for his week's supply of water. He also had another name, but we knew this old man simply as "The Bachelor." He lived a rather lonely existence in a little shack no more than 12′ x 14′, where he sharpened tools for a living.

The bachelor's song reminded me that it would soon be time for the Good Deed Club on the radio. Our temperamental radio needed some patient coaxing until those unforgettable strains of "Do-o a good deed every day, obey the golden rule, never say an angry word or be unkind or cruel" would be heard. This was followed by interminable tap dancing, and of course the highlight of the program, the 21-jewel-gold watch that was awarded to the good deeder of the week from Eaton's. I could always stretch my job of furniture waxing in the living room exactly until the program was over.

This being Saturday, we were worried about Dad getting home from the store in time for the Christmas program in church. He usually closed a little later than the Red and White across the street, because then we would get their customers. And when he finally would come he would bring Japanese oranges and of course the Mexican roasted peanuts from the 100 lb sack in the corner, for which the bargain store was famous. Why, people came from Winnipeg just to buy their Christmas peanuts at our store. I never have been able to get quite such good peanuts since.

Anyway, after our baths, with our skin all tingly and itchy, partly from the hard water and partly from the homemade soap and partly from nervous excitement, we would stand by the stove and proceed to brush the tangles out of our long hair. And then we would don our Christmas clothes and get even more goose pimply and itchy.

As Mom did last minute hemming, we would practise our "pieces." Out of sheer necessity to retain her sanity, or maybe Mom's gift for thinking of the less fortunate, she would send two or three of us over to the bachelor's with some fresh buns and peppernuts. Leaving the complete confusion of our hectic household and jumping over the caragana hedges, we entered the desolation and solitude of that little shack. It smelled not of spruce trees on this special day, but like it always smelled: a little misty, a mixture of tobacco juice, liniment and peppermint. But today there was a twinkle in his eyes, and his appearance, what with his white hair and beard, was not unlike that of the "Nate Kloss" (St. Nick) he spoke of. And we were brave enough, Marina and I, to recite our verses to him, unbidden. For this we received a peppermint each and we scooted home, glad to be back in a normal chaotic household once again. The inevitable had happened! The tree, the best one we had ever had, had come crashing down, in all of its Christmas finery! I remember Tina yelling at Peter for the rest of that day. I guess it must have been his fault.

Memories of the Last Day Before Christmas

Grace Warkentin's mother and sisters. From left to right: Marj, Mother Maria, Leona, Amanda, Helen, Kathryn, Mary, LaVerna, Betty, Grace, and Marina. Photo credit: Grace Warkentin.

It was a good thing that the Sunday School teachers had saved my place in the bench, because we were always a little late. During the program, if I got too fidgety before my part, I could always busy myself by pulling the basting threads out of the hem of my new dress.

And finally, when it was all over and the last *tutjes* (bags) had been distributed, I remember walking home in that crisp Christmas evening. As I passed the show-hall and the creamery, the strings of lights across Main Street stopped. But, oh the wonder of it, God had taken over with His own showy display! The northern lights cascaded gloriously across the sky in the form of a giant pipe organ. With the vivid crescendo of rise and fall it seemed as though Someone was swelling forth the majestic anthem, "Jesus Christ is born this day." I was fairly bursting with the ecstasy of that wondrous sight to end this full day of sights, sounds, smells and sensations. I skipped on homeward and past the pump to offer my personal thank you to God for His great Love.

I am grown up now, but that pump, now painted a glossy silver, still stands there as a reminder of my childhood. And I know it would take more than five strong pumps of the handle to prompt any water from its spout.

Winnipeg's Portage Avenue at Christmas (1956).

The Unknown Santa: Silver Dollar Is His Trademark

Winnipeg Tribune, December 24, 1958

In the 1940s and '50s, Winnipeg had its own Secret Santa by the name of Morris Duchov. Every year, he would enlist a legion of helpers to deliver gifts to children around the city without fanfare or publicity. Although he died in 1956, his generosity continues to this day with an endowment fund in his name at the Winnipeg Foundation.

LMOST ANY NEWSPAPERMAN COULD have written this story years ago. But nobody did.

Who wants to be on the wrong side of Santa Claus?

And Morris Duchov as every newspaperman and every radio broadcaster knew was a modern Santa.

For years he enjoyed his anonymous role but suddenly he died. Maybe it's time to let other people enjoy it, too.

He was known to a vast number of Winnipeggers as the proprietor of the popular O-Kum Inn on Carlton Street. But he never allowed his thriving business to take up all of his time. He never forgot Christmas and he attempted to extend its spirit the whole year round.

This Christmas Eve, two years after his death, the spirit of Morris Duchov will pay its annual visit to Manitoba's orphanages and hospitals where children are confined.

His symbol was a silver dollar which some 200 children received every year, together with countless other gifts of Christmas cheer. Morris didn't want any child to be forgotten and he called on his friends in the newspaper and radio fields to be his helpers.

They were honoured to perform such a cheerful task. They would talk about it among themselves for months after Christmas and marvel at the blunt-spoken little man who made it all possible.

The man who never delivered the gifts himself would sit back in his easy chair, after the deliveries were made, and listen to his helpers tell of the happy faces they had seen.

That was the sum total of the reporting of the Duchov Christmas party, a sort of itemized summary of goodness itself, to be entered in the ledger at the North Pole.

The real headquarters of this unrecorded Christmas party was Duchov's tiny apartment in the Bettes Block, just across the street from his restaurant. Crowded into the small living room, its corners packed high with more cartons to be delivered on Christmas Day itself, the helpers would return to cross-check on additional deliveries.

Duchov's obvious enjoyment was rewarded enough but his spirit demanded that friendship itself should be saluted at such a time, with cigars, food and a modest approach to the wassail bowl which contained a full measure of Duchov's enthusiasm.

Morris Duchov's Christmas list grew year upon year: St. Agnes School, St. Joseph's, The Children's Aid Society, Knowles', Centre Winnipeg Boys' Club and the Shriners' hospital. Each gift was addressed specifically to boy or girl and each had Morris' traditional gift—a silver dollar—taped to the top of each box.

"Only someone who understood children would have added the silver dollar," said one hospital official. "Somehow it made it a special gift."

"We never saw him at the hospital," said a Shriners' Hospital official. "The first year the gifts arrived, the man who delivered them simply refused to tell us who had donated them. Later, when we found out who it was, we invited him to our Christmas party but he never came."

Rev. Fred Douglas, of St. Andrew's United Church, remembers the first Christmas the dollar-tagged boxes arrived at the Centre Winnipeg Boy's Club. Morris had heard of the club from his many friends on the city police force who were his agents for finding more places where help was needed.

"We had about 150 boys in the club and I thought someone ought to thank Mr. Duchov, but the men who brought the gifts said he wouldn't like it," recalled Mr. Douglas. "After it happened the second time, I decided to visit his restaurant but he refused to talk about what he had done. I ended up by telling him all about what we were doing at the club."

"He never would discuss it with anyone," said a police officer who helped Duchov, "but he didn't save it all for Christmas, you know. He was always willing to help anybody, but particularly children. He provided more than 20 television sets to children at institutions, to my knowledge."

Several years before he died, Duchov set up the Press-Radio Scholarship Fund for Orphans. He made the large initial donation and the fund was bolstered by a bequest from his estate. The fund supports 11 orphans this year in their quest for higher education. One year when a particularly deserving orphan had to be omitted because of stiff competition and limited funds, Duchov simply handed a blank cheque to the committee operating the fund.

The Unknown Santa

And so it went on, the unknown life of Morris Duchov who came to Canada as an orphan himself out of the turmoil of the Russian revolution. A man, who lost his parents while still a child, who had no family of his own in Winnipeg, he began his successful restaurant business as a pedlar of soft drinks and sandwiches to the newsroom at *The Tribune*.

That was the beginning of his long friendship with newspapermen which he carried to Carlton Street when he opened his restaurant beside *The Free Press*. Newspapermen, radio announcers and policemen were the nucleus of his successful business which was just to be expanded into another restaurant beside the new Post Office when he suddenly died, while still in his 40s.

Persons who knew Morris Duchov wouldn't want to forget him. That's why, come this Christmas Eve, newspapermen, radio announcers and some policemen will be out again on Duchov's duty, carrying parcels to a long list of children.

The gifts are paid for by the many persons who knew Morris and, if the bank has a big enough supply on hand, the children will receive on the top of each box Morris' symbol—the silver dollar.

And as some newspaperman helper hands a tot her gift he may well say:

"Yes, Virginia, there was a Morris Duchov."

Hudson Bay Mining & Smelting Staff House, Flin Flon.

The Spirit of Christmas

Margaret V. Fast
Whitewater Lake, 1961

Margaret Fast's name may be familiar to some Manitobans. She has had a long career in public health and was formerly the medical officer of health for Winnipeg. In her story, Margaret recollects one memorable Christmas when her community came together to help her family after her father became ill.

OUR FARM WAS NESTLED on the edge of the Whitewater marsh, deep inside southwestern Manitoba. On a map you might need to look for Whitewater Lake, since the marsh did become a lake some years. Two other farms were a part of our little corner of the world: Harold and May and their two children lived at the very end of the road and Bill and Edna lived across the road from us. Although they were both "English" and part of the English community and we were Mennonite and part of the originally-German-speaking Mennonite community, we all got along very well.

In November of 1961, the marsh and the farms were already blanketed with snow; I don't remember a November when that was not the case. It was a part of the Christmas tradition.

Another part of the Christmas tradition was that we would all be together. My older brothers, both studying in the city, would come home and join our parents and our two younger sisters.

Misfortune came quickly and unexpectedly.

"I am feeling awful," said Dad as he came in from the barn that Saturday and slumped down in his usual chair beside the bookcase in the kitchen. "My chest hurts, my arm hurts; I'm so tired." He was having trouble breathing and rivulets of sweat ran down his face. Dad was never, ever sick. Farm work was hard. He'd rest a bit and then he'd be off to finish the chores.

Then my mom, who couldn't drive, was on the phone. "May? George is really sick. He needs to get to the doctor. Can you take him?"

Fear crept into our house that day and it did not leave for a very long time. Perhaps it never entirely left. But, initially, it was a wraith that lurked only in the corners of our minds. Everything really would be fine. It had to be. But of course, it wasn't. Anyone reading that list of symptoms today will know that Dad was having a heart attack. As it turned out, a massive heart attack. He was in hospital until after Christmas.

My brothers borrowed a car and drove to Boissevain for a day to visit Dad. Then, they returned to Winnipeg and Mom and three girls, ages 15, 13 and seven, were left to manage the farm. Mom, with some help from the girls, traditionally did the "inside" work, cooking, cleaning, canning, baking bread, churning butter, hauling water, doing laundry, and so much more and Dad did most of the "outside" work.

That Christmas season, we could not have managed without the kindness of neighbours and of our community. Our church community volunteered/conscripted their young sons, generally about my age or a few years older, to spend a week at a time on the farm working with me and Mom to get the farm work done: milk the cows, muck out the barn, feed the animals and look after all the myriad tasks of a mixed farm. Fortunately, high schools in the province had been regionalized a few years previously and the lads and I were able to take the school bus to the high school in Boissevain.

It was our neighbours, Harold and May, however, who drove my younger sisters to the local school for all those weeks. Their son also attended the school but it meant all the driving, twice a day, was up to them.

That Christmas was poignant. I don't recall that there were many presents under the tree but we had managed, with a lot of help, to keep the farm going; the boys were home for a few weeks; and Dad was expected home soon. We did not yet know how irrevocably our lives had been changed by the event of that November day. On that Christmas Day we were all simply very grateful.

Oh Christmas Tree!

Petrosha
Near Dauphin, 1964

Gunfire isn't usually associated with Christmas tree cutting, but it was one year when seven-year old Petrosha was an unwitting accomplice in a "tree poaching" episode. This story was previously published on Petrosha's blog, petroshasblog.wordpress.com and is reprinted with permission.

Y EARLIEST RECOLLECTION OF Christmas is when I was seven years old. As you read this, let's see if I can take you back to an adventure of mine so many years ago.

My brother, who had a way of getting me into all sorts of interesting situations (a.k.a. trouble), and I got dressed in our warmest winter clothes and headed out the door in search of a tree.

It was a cold prairie afternoon. We were dressed in knit sweaters under our parkas. On our feet we wore Dad's grey wool socks inside our black high-top rubber boots. This particular day, we had two pairs of mittens on our hands. Our toques were pulled down to our eyes and the scarves were pulled over our mouths all the way up to our noses. No skin exposed except for the slits for our eyes! Our warm breath caused a puff of steam to rise out of the scarves. Icicles would form on the wool in just a matter of seconds!

With a small hatchet in hand, our sheet-metal sleigh and our dog, Snoopy, my brother and I headed out that day to the very back of our property. We walked on top of at least three feet of crispy hard packed snow. If we were lucky we wouldn't break through and sink up to our waists! Snoopy of course took giant leaps and crashed through, only to emerge a few feet ahead of us. I remember how only the top of her head could be seen bounding along through the snow banks. She loved coming out with us on our adventures.

There was a barb-wire fence at the back of our yard and we had to be careful crawling in between the wires to get through. The snow-covered ground went on for acres and was as flat as could be. No one had recently walked out here and there were no animal tracks either. Sometimes we saw rabbits and even coyotes out here. But not today.

We continued on until we came to the "bush" as I called it. This forested area was beside a deep ravine and it was dense with shrubs. There were lots of young spruce trees growing in amongst the poplar and maple trees. We looked around for a bit and found a tree that was the right size and shape for our family's living room. We chopped it down. We didn't waste any time out there because we were hot and sweaty from all that walking and we were now getting cold. It was also starting to get dark outside. We loaded up the tree and headed for home.

Now this is the part I really remember well. As we were almost back to the barbwire fence and our property, someone in the distance yelled out at us. My brother told me to hurry because we could get shot at! And yes, just as we scrambled back through the fence, pulling the sleigh with our prize tree, loud shots from a shotgun were heard. Whether or not any buckshot came flying at us, we never knew. The two of us were running as fast as we could, breaking through the snow, falling and sinking. But we kept on moving. Not to worry about Snoopy however, as she was a smart dog and was way ahead of us as we all ran for home!

As you can guess, we had chopped down a tree from someone's property. He lived in an old brick house in that bush and was known around the town as a grouchy old man. My brother had nicknamed him Bela Lugosi back then and it was only recently that I figured out why.

I remember that Christmas tree well. It had been four years since a tree had been set up at our house. It was the first Christmas that I recall growing up as a child.

That Christmas, we had the tree with the old glass ornaments and coloured lights. Straw was put under the dinner table and candles were lit to welcome our guests. We had lots of relatives over for dinner. We ate kutia, borscht, perogies and cabbage rolls. Uncle Metro's family gave us a box of chocolates. In return, Uncle got a pack of cigarettes from us. I received one memorable gift. It was a fuzzy brown store-bought sweater.

Why do I remember all this so clearly? You see, when I was three years old, my eldest sister had passed away. Thinking back, it had been so very hard on my parents. Our home was very sad for a long time. We never talked about it when I was young, but I now believe that after those four years of sadness, our real tree that year helped to restore faith and happiness in our home at Christmas time.

Not sure whose idea it was to get that real tree that year. But I'm glad we did.

Finnish Christmas Traditions

Trish Suzanne
Port Arthur, Ontario, 1960s

Although Trish Suzanne's story actually takes place in Northwestern Ontario, I have included it in this anthology because her grandparents had lived in Manitoba for many years, where her grandfather worked as a CNR foreman in various railway towns and settlements. They decided to retire to Port Arthur (now Thunder Bay) because of its large Finnish community. Trish reminiscences about Christmastime visits to her grandparents' home and the unique Finnish custom of running into a snowbank to cool off from a hot sauna!

CHRISTMAS EVE WAS A special time. We would sit around my grandparents' kitchen table, hungry from our long travelled journey from Winnipeg to Port Arthur, Ontario. My grandmother would prepare a light meal consisting of rye crispbread, tilsit cheese, pickled herring, and her delicious homemade head cheese, which is a jelled meat made from pig's feet. For dessert we ate my grandmother's Finnish coffee bread and pink cranberry pudding, as well as what seemed like an unlimited amount of Japanese oranges and Christmas ribbon candy which was kept in my grandparents' copper tinder box.

I remember, on several occasions, when my grandparents adorned their Christmas tree with tiny wax candles. While family members watched attentively, the candles were set aglow. Although this was a time-honoured tradition, it frightened me to think how easily it could have ended in disaster.

My grandmother wanted us to open our presents on Christmas Eve, while my mother liked us to wait until Christmas morning. They would compromise, where upon we were each allowed to open one gift before going to bed. Taking our newly unwrapped toy into bed with us made falling to sleep a difficult undertaking.

Christmas morning was spent exchanging and opening gifts. In the afternoon, we would burn off our abundance of excess energy tobogganing down the big hill behind our grandparents' house. By early evening we were feasting on a sumptuous turkey dinner, followed by a visit to an invitingly warm and very relaxing sauna which was located in a separate building in my grandparents' back yard.

Sometimes, several overheated, daring members of my family would rush out of the sauna and plunge naked, into the closest snowbank. It was a great way to cool off and definitely a Finnish Christmas tradition.

Donna Gamache's parents, Ronald and Evelyn Firby, the recipients of the gift in her story. Donna dedicates the story to their memory. Photo courtesy of Donna Gamache.

A Christmas to Remember

Donna Firby Gamache
Near Minnedosa, 1966

Most of us can relate to Donna Gamache's story of trying to find the perfect gift for someone, and the great pleasure in seeing that your efforts were appreciated.

IN OUR BASEMENT SITS an old stereo cabinet, no longer used for music, but still serving as a convenient place to put items. And it still brings back memories, especially of one special Christmas.

The year was 1966—the year I finished university and began my first teaching job a hundred miles from home. It was the year I finally had money to buy presents that I'd wanted to give for years, but couldn't afford.

I began to shop in early November, starting small with stocking stuffers, toys and trinkets for my nephews. As the Christmas season neared, as stores became crowded and holiday music blared from loudspeakers, I turned to larger items, for my brother, sister and brother-in-law. I left my parents' gift until last.

There was no doubt what that gift should be. For years, I'd longed to give them a stereo—not a small, portable record player such as I owned, but a real stereo of walnut or oak, a fine piece of wood to grace their living room.

My parents—grain and cattle farmers—loved music, but I knew they would never spend money on such an item, even if they could afford it. I pictured Dad relaxing in his chair after evening chores, while Perry Como crooned a tune. I could almost hear Mother singing along with the old Christmas carols, especially her favourite, "O Little Town of Bethlehem."

I began to frequent music and furniture stores, asking questions, but not yet buying, for there was one major problem. I could not buy the stereo in the town where I worked, nor in a larger centre, because of the difficulty of having it delivered at an appropriate time. The logical place was my hometown, but arrangements might be tricky. I wanted the stereo to be a surprise, and I wanted to be home when it arrived.

Fortunately, I was able to drive home for a weekend early in December. I left the moment Friday classes ended. I could manage half an hour to shop and still arrive at the farm at my usual time.

Luck was on my side. The town's only furniture store had a lovely model of the type I wanted. It was expensive, but within my means. I bought it on the spot, after promises that it would be delivered on the day before Christmas, at whatever time I telephoned them to come. By then, I should be home for the holidays, and I would try to have my parents out of the house for a while.

On the afternoon before Christmas, they decided to drive into town for some last-minute groceries. I had been counting on that. The moment their car turned at the end of our lane, I was on the phone.

An hour later the delivery truck arrived, and the movers unloaded the stereo into our living room. I'd rearranged furniture to give it a prominent spot.

When Mom and Dad returned, the sound of Perry Como singing Christmas carols met them at the door. The look on their faces, when they saw the source of the music, was something I'll always remember.

The Christmas stereo cabinet. Photo credit: Donna Gamache.

Guess Who's Coming to Dinner?

Roger Currie
Winnipeg, 1967

Veteran broadcaster Roger Currie recalls one Christmas when he was a college student and invited a friend home for Christmas dinner. Words like "awkward" and "tense" come to mind in describing what transpired at the dinner table.

THE YEAR WAS 1967. I was a student at St. John's College at the University of Manitoba. I lived a very comfortable life with my family in River Heights, driving my mother's car and paying a ridiculously small tuition compared to what today's students are burdened with. Most homes in our neighbourhood could have been right out of *Leave it to Beaver* or *Father Knows Best*. Mom stayed home, and at Christmas time she organized a festive dinner for what we affectionately called "the geriatric club." In the 1950s, that "club" included my three surviving grandparents, a step-grandmother, a widowed great aunt and a great uncle who was a widower.

Roger Currie

While my older brother and I dove into our Christmas treasures, playing with the latest hockey board game in the pre-digital era, Mother spent the entire day in the kitchen it seemed. There were no microwaves or automatic dishwashers. When he wasn't chauffeuring the geriatrics, our dear old dad was wearing an apron, with a dish towel over his shoulder. But as head of the household, he firmly decreed that absolutely everything stopped in the morning when the Queen's Christmas broadcast came on the radio. When it was finally served, the Christmas feast was truly grand and very traditional. There was a beautifully stuffed turkey, mashed potatoes with perfect gravy, boiled onions in a cream sauce and tomato aspic with shrimp. Dessert included endless shortbread, mince tarts and a steaming plum pudding with two different sugary sauces.

No one dreamed of asking for anything gluten-free. It was long before food banks were even contemplated. No doubt there were many people in Winnipeg who didn't have anything like we had, but they tended to be "out of sight and out of mind." We just didn't think about them very much. There was not an abundance of alcohol served at the Currie Christmas, partly out of deference to my grandfather the dentist who was a lifelong teetotaller. But once the older folks were out the door, mother would kick off her ridiculous high heels and knock back a couple of rather stiff gins. Dad was probably still in the kitchen drying and polishing dishes, while nibbling leftovers.

By 1967, the Christmas cast had changed somewhat. Gone to the great seniors home in the sky were two of the grandparents and the great uncle. But feisty Aunt Marie was still with us, along with Grandma Currie with her delightful Glasgow accent that she brought with her to Canada in 1910, a year before she gave birth to our father in Brandon.

Aunt Marie was a Swede from Hallock, Minnesota. Today, she might easily be described as a "bigot." Lord knows if she were here now, she might be supporting someone like Donald Trump! Forty-nine years ago, Marie was fairly "representative" of her generation. Did I mention that she loved to talk, and rather loudly?

The devil seems to have played a role in my entry into the world in 1947. As far back as I can remember, I have always taken something of a "guilty pleasure" in "stirring the pot" to make day-to-day life a bit more interesting. In 1967, I conspired to liven up our Yuletide feast by inviting a "person of colour" to share our table.

He was a University colleague whose name was Fitzroy Clarke. He came from the island of St. Vincent in the Caribbean, and like many foreign students he was destined to be thousands of miles from home and pretty much alone at Christmas.

We gave no advance warning that Fitzroy would be joining us. Polite greetings were exchanged, a suitable blessing was shared as we bowed our heads, and dinner was served.

None of us could remember Aunt Marie ever having so little to say at a family gathering, but the expression on her face spoke volumes. Our Caribbean guest held forth on a wide range of topics. He was not the least bit shy. My older brother David who was visiting from Toronto, laughed heartily through all of it, shooting me many a knowing glance and a wink.

The passage of so many years has dimmed the memory of what exactly might have been said that evening. The only people still around today are my brother and me, and hopefully Fitzroy Clarke. In recent years I've tried Google and other digital means to find him, without success.

My fondest wish is that he returned to St. Vincent or some other tropical paradise and continues to enjoy a truly wonderful life. He certainly helped create some wonderful Christmas memories at our house in Winnipeg in 1967.

Sadly, Roger found out recently that Fitzroy Clarke had passed away in 2003, at the age of 56.

Santa visiting children in Lord Selkirk Park in Winnipeg, 1968.

Time-lapse photo of holiday lights along Winnipeg's Portage Avenue, ca. 1970s-80s.

My Best Present? My Brother

Theresa Oswald
Winnipeg, 1973

Former MLA and provincial minister Theresa Oswald writes about a special Christmas Eve when she was stuck at home with the flu, but her big brother decided to stay with her instead of going to a Christmas party.

I REMEMBER THAT HOLIDAY season very well, despite it being more than a few years ago. I was seven years old and battling a loathsome cold and flu, accompanied by a debilitating earache that I was prone to have in those early years of life. I was, in short, not fit for prime time.

Our Christmas Eve tradition was to travel two streets over to Auntie Pat's and Uncle Don's home to admire their tree, eat my aunt's famous butter tarts and enjoy fun and frivolity with our young cousins. I was crestfallen at the prospect of having to stay home and miss the party and, to be fair, so were my parents.

My brother, Brad Oswald (yes, your favourite TV critic, same guy), swiftly stepped in and encouraged Mom and Dad to go for a few hours and enjoy themselves, and that he would stay home with "the patient."

It is important to note that Brad would have been 15 years old at the time. That's right. A teenage boy volunteering to miss great food and good fun so he could care for his little sister. He gave my parents a familiar smile that said, "Don't worry, I've got this," and reluctantly, they departed.

Brad gave me fluids and medicine and cookies and milk. He fluffed my pillow and covered me with my favourite blanket. Together we watched *The Grinch Who Stole Christmas*, to which he sang along enthusiastically. He read some of my most beloved Christmas books, complete with all the goofy voices.

Just before bedtime, he constructed the most enormous and spectacular stocking (made out of green garbage bags, no joke) and put it in place of my pretty, but comparatively minuscule regular sock. I was sure Santa could fit a hippopotamus into that thing, if he so chose. It was absolutely glorious, and I know I fell asleep that night without a thought of searing pain in my ear or wretched infection in my chest.

I couldn't tell you anything about the gifts I received the next morning, best, worst or otherwise. The truth is, Santa hadn't much of a chance of topping the Christmas magic that happened for me the night before. It turns out, Brad, that the best present ever wasn't a present at all. It was you.

All my love at Christmas, and every day, —Theresa

The family tradition continues: Leah Boulet's husband and children getting the family tree. Watercolour and photo by Leah Boulet.

A Charlie Brown Tree

Leah Boulet
Pine Falls, 1978

Leah Boulet shares a story about searching for the perfect Christmas tree with her father, Marcel Pitre, who is also a contributor to this anthology. She wrote about this memory many years later and presented it to him as a special Christmas gift.

I REMEMBER WHEN I was young I loved to go into the bush with you and pick out our Christmas tree. Each year you started up the old, yellow snowmobile and hitched on the sled to cart the tree home. I'd jump on the seat behind you and off we'd roar into the snow-covered forest, cold wind nipping at our faces.

One year the hitch broke so you couldn't attach the sled. *How are we going to get the tree home?* I thought as we pulled away from the house and zipped up the trail to our favourite tree hunting spot. You cut the engine and I heard the muffled silence of a winter day in the bush. Axe in hand, we tramped through snow up to our knees. Each tall-standing evergreen required serious consideration. Then we found it—a perfect tree. With a few swift strokes of the axe the tree toppled to the ground. You trimmed the branches, and cut off the top and bottom. The rough scent of pine and cut wood perfumed the air. Our tree was ready to go, but how? It was too big to put across our laps.

"You sit facing the back of the snowmobile, Leah, and hold onto the trunk of the tree. I'll drive slowly and we'll drag it home," you said. I gulped, sat backwards on the seat behind you, and grabbed hold of the tree with both mitten-clad hands. A few brown birds chirped and scattered from a nearby dogwood tree as the roar of the snowmobile cut the quiet. We inched forward at a snail's pace. A carpet of green needles trailed behind us. Each bump in the trail felt like a mountain. I gripped my knees hard against the sides of the seat to keep from falling off. My arms started to shake, and an ache crawled up from my hands, past my elbows, and into my shoulders. The ache turned into a jabbing pain. Gritting my teeth, I held on tighter and tighter until I thought my fingers would break. My world narrowed to the whine of the machine and the green burden bumping and twisting in my hands. Minutes became hours. A ten minute ride lasted a year. Then we were home. Finally!

Exhausted, I flopped onto the snow bank beside the driveway. A chill seeped through my nylon parka, cooling down my overheated body. You grabbed the tree and stood it up for inspection. Our beautiful tree! It was full of holes and broken branches! Disappointment washed over me. I rolled over and buried my face into the cold snow. I wanted to cry. "Hey," you exclaimed, "it looks like a Charlie Brown tree!" I flipped back and slid off the snow bank. You were right! It looked exactly like the tree in the Charlie Brown Christmas cartoon. I grinned and wiped the wet from my cheeks. From then on, a Charlie Brown tree stood with pride in our home each year we found a tree together.

Making a Charlie Brown Christmas tree. Drawing by Leah Boulet.

The Christmas Wreath

Wayne Chan
Winnipeg, late 1970s

My own modest contribution to the anthology isn't a heartwarming, "Chicken Soup for the Soul" kind of tale, but I think it illustrates some of the amusing culture clashes that can occur in ethnic families.

Many of my fondest memories of Christmas are associated with school activities. The busy preparation and excitement leading up to the school Christmas concert, the rehearsals and choir practices, and the holiday craft projects. To this day, I still have a couple of festive handicrafts that I made as a child.

One year in elementary school (I can't recall which grade it was now), we had to make a Christmas wreath from a metal coat hanger and some strips from a plastic garbage bag. The coat hanger was bent into a circle and the plastic strips would be tied to it to form a wreath. Our teacher told us to bring a coat hanger and some green garbage bags, and if we didn't have any green bags, white ones would do.

At home, we didn't have any green garbage bags, but we did have some of the smaller white ones, so I brought those to class, along with the coat hanger. The craft project went off without a hitch and I had a beautiful snowy white Christmas wreath at the end of it. On my way home, I had visions of it being proudly displayed on our front door.

In those early years, my grandparents lived with us, and there were eight of us under one roof, which is hard to imagine now. Although my grandfather and my parents had been in Canada for many years, my grandmother was only able to join the rest of the family much later. She was a very traditional person and continued to observe many of the folk customs of old China even after coming to Canada.

I tugged the wreath out of my knapsack with both hands and presented it to my grandmother.

Rather than the high praise I was expecting for my handiwork, I got:

"AAAAAAAAAAAAAAAAAAAAH!"

She went into hysterics and told me in no uncertain terms to get "it" out of her bedroom!

The situation didn't improve when my parents came home in the evening. My dad asked how I could be so crazy as to make such a thing and what the heck were they teaching us kids these days. All and sundry demanded that the wreath be physically removed from the house.

And it was thus that my beautiful snowy white wreath ended up in the trash can in the garage.

Needless to say, I was rather disconcerted by the whole affair. My memory is a little hazy on what happened next, but I seem to recall that my mom relented and allowed me to go and retrieve my poor little wreath, as long as I kept it out of sight. I didn't dare bring it back into the house, so I hung it in the garage, where I stood in the cold air and admired it for a while. I'm not sure what I did with it later, but I'm pretty sure didn't throw it away like I was supposed to. I think it became a shell-game of "hide the wreath" when grown-ups were around.

It wasn't until long afterwards that I learned why everyone was in such an uproar over a plastic wreath. Little did I know at the time (since no one had ever explained it to me), that the colour of mourning in China was white. I was essentially giving a funeral wreath to my dear, aged grandmother!

North of the Highway

Erin Hammond
Bakers Narrows, 1980s

Erin Hammond fondly recalls Christmases with her family at Bakers Narrows in northern Manitoba. Her story first appeared in Cottage North *magazine in 2003 and is reprinted with permission.*

SOME SAY THAT "YOU can never go home again." These people say that once you leave the nest to pursue your own career and pay your own bills, it is infinitely impossible to feel fully comfortable in your parents' home. Well ... these people have never lived at Bakers Narrows.

As far back as I can remember our family was at the lake. I remember waking up in my bed on a beautiful summer day, and relishing the moment. I would lay there for a minute, without moving, and just listen. Listen to the song of the whippoorwill, and to the way the summer breeze would move the trees in the back yard. I remember feeling SO free. All that consumed my mind was the water. I couldn't wait to get myself down to the lake, so that my day of imagining and playing could begin. I would eventually stumble out into the hallway that overlooked our sunken living room, and I would look out the large windows onto the lake. If it was motionless and tranquil, and you couldn't tell where the water stopped and the sky started, then I knew that it was going to be a beautiful day north of the highway on Lake Athapapuskow.

My brother Evan and I, and some other children at the lake, spent our days in the wilderness. Whether it was swimming or exploring, we were always outside. From sunrise to sundown, and sometimes even beyond, we played. We played in the water, we played in the bush. We made mud pies and played in the sandbox, and when we got hungry, we went next door to Grandma and Grandpa's place. I remember being in the lake and smelling homemade bread and Grandma's famous split-pea soup, and running up from the lake to indulge. Evan and I would sit on lawn chairs, with the water running down our legs and dripping off of our toes onto the Astroturf-covered deck, and Grandma would chat us up about some really interesting, unknown part of her life. I remember thinking that she was such a neat lady, and wondering what she did when she was my age. When she was called in from playing, what did her grandma make her for lunch?

The worst part of lunch, however, was always when Grandma told us that we could not go back into the water for at least thirty minutes after eating. I remember thinking, even at that young age, "What's the worst that can happen ... a tummy ache? I can handle that!!" I remember swearing to myself, right then and there, that I would

NEVER tell my children that, EVER. I still remember the way my bathing suit looked up close in those days, as I walked down to the beach with my head hung down, mumbling to myself of how I would never make my children suffer as Grandma had made Evan and I. It's funny how serious I was about that. It's funny how serious kids are about a lot of things.

We were one of the first families to live out at Bakers Narrows not only in the summer, but in the winter as well. I have such vivid memories of not agreeing with the decision that my parents had made about living at the lake year-round, because I was in grade nine at this point and really wanted to be able to spend time with my friends in town. Mom and Dad, however, went out of their way to make sure that they accommodated all of my and Evan's activities, and when the time came, they generously supplied us with vehicles of our own.

Over time, I began to enjoy being at the lake in the winter. Having a car of my own (which was older than Evan was), I could have a part-time job and see my friends when I wanted to, and I could also come home to the lake where I had peace and quiet for homework, writing, or rest. Mom and Dad bought two snow machines when I was in high school and that was fun, but rather short-lived. I wrapped one of them around a tree a few too many times, and suddenly it was "traded in" for something else, like a snow-blower or a lawnmower. I think Dad got tired of me walking home in tears from deep in the bush, and having to listen to me tell him the whole story of where I left his really expensive investment.

If it wasn't snowmobiling, then it was something else. We could go ice fishing with the Ayers' kids next door, or just play some shinny on the lake where Dad would make a rink. And sometimes, when we were feeling rather enthusiastic, we would tie the toboggan behind the car and pull it around in the park. I remember being scared that I was going to smack into a tree or something, but it never happened. Those were the good old days ... when rules were not nearly as important as having fun.

And after all this was said and done, we would go inside and take the layers and layers of clothes off downstairs in the basement, and then go upstairs in our long underwear and socks (that were hanging off our feet from pulling them out of our boots) to warm up. Dad would light a fire and we would sit in front of the stunning brick fireplace that he and Grandpa Hammond made, and Mom would bring us some hot chocolate.

There was nothing like the feeling of being active in the pure, beautiful wilderness, and then coming in to feel such safety and warmth with my family. We would sit under a blanket that was handmade by someone who loved us, and we would watch "Hockey Night in Canada." At that point, I didn't realize what a special gift that would turn out to be.

North of the Highway

The most special time at the lake in the winter has always been Christmas, and it has been even more so in the last couple of years since I have lived elsewhere. I have been gone for close to ten years, and once Christmas hits the stores and the radios in the city, I feel a yearning to go home ... to go north. It is ironic how when I now walk through the decorated malls and department stores that I wished I had as a teen, I feel such a deep sense of ache for the cottage.

At Christmas, our house was full of the smells of sweet shortbread and clove-stuffed oranges. We always wished for snow, so that we could look out of our window and see huge snowflakes falling onto the lake. Late at night, we would put on our boots and go out onto the ice, so that we could stand together and look at our beautiful tree and its shimmering lights through our windows. I remember standing there with my family, drinking in the awesome smell of smoke coming out of the chimney, and hoping that my wish-list arrived at the North Pole many months before.

Now, as I age, my parents still wait for me to come home before they will put up our tree. We have a tradition in our house that my dad and I go out into the bush together to find the perfect tree. We drive together in the truck and talk about the things that count in life, and the things that we are thankful for. And EVERY year that we do this, we find *the* tree and we carry that tree out of the bush, and take it home to put up in the house. And every year, we feel a deep connection to our family. Not only to our immediate family, but to our family that has passed on, and to our family that is too far away for us to be able to share a cider and laugh with around the tree.

Christmas has always been, and still remains, a very special place at the Hammond cottage. There is not a lot of room in the house, so Christmas is usually a busy, loud, fun time. Friends and families come over, and we spend a lot of time laughing in pleasant nostalgia and sharing the new experiences of our lives with each other. There is never a dull moment, and we are always aware of how wonderful we have it.

Christmas at our house has never been fancy, but it has always been magical. Over the last couple of years, my favourite thing to do when all of the guests have left and there is nothing on but the lights of the Christmas tree, is to lie on the bed and look out the skylight window. All that I can hear is the crackling of the warm fire at my feet, and the north wind through the trees. And all that I can see are the stars in the sky through the branches of evergreens, and the occasional northern lights. And sometimes I swear, even at this age, that if I look hard enough, I will see a sleigh pulled by reindeer flying past my window, filled with presents and a whole lot of love.

It has taken my being away from Flin Flon and the lake to be able to see how much I love it, and how much it is vital to who I am as an individual. I have also realized over the last couple of years that my mom and dad tried to give Evan and me freedom, by offering us a childhood full of imagination and exploration. It was in this freedom that I learned valuable lessons as a child that helped me to grow into a strong-willed, independent adult with a sense of responsibility and appreciation for the world that God has made. Experiences like walking to the lodge with no shoes on and, as my feet burned hot on the tar, I realized that I had made a poor decision; getting permission to take the boat out and show off to all my friends without checking to see if there was gas in the tank; playing baseball in the back yard VERY close to the windows.

It's funny how, no matter how old I get, I can still remember EXACT moments. Like the way it felt to go for that last swim of the day, when the sun had just gone down, and to then come in for a snack in my pyjamas before bed. Or the way it felt to have a big, fat pickerel on the end of my line, on a gorgeous day in the boat. Like the way I felt when I saw Grandpa Watson dressed as Santa come in the door at Grandma and Grandpa's house. I remember these exact moments sometimes to the point that it hurts.

I have heard some parents say that they work their whole lives to give their children what they could not have. What I know is that I want to work throughout my life to give my children what I DID have. Summer in the water. Christmas in the snow. Such wonderful memories at the cottage. In essence: Beauty. So yes ... as far as this "lake girl" is concerned, you can go home again.

Memories of Christmases Past

Brandy Reid
Cranberry Portage, 1980s–90s

Flin Flon blogger Brandy Reid writes about her family's Christmas traditions when she was growing up in Cranberry Portage, and her hopes of starting new holiday traditions with her own kids. A version of this story was previously published on her blog, myunwrittenlife.com, and is reprinted with permission.

THE OTHER NIGHT BEFORE bed I was thinking about what Christmas was like when I was growing up.

I so wish that my boys could have grown up the way I did. Or moreover, with the traditions we had, especially at Christmas time.

It would all start with hunting for a Christmas tree. My dad owns a sawmill with his brother and every year we would drive down the road leading to the sawmill looking for the perfect tree. We would bundle up in our ski-pants, winter jacket, boots, mitts, toques, and scarves. It never failed—it always seemed to be the coldest day of winter when Dad took us out to look for a tree.

Most often Dad would have already scoped a tree out in the past few weeks. However, when we would get close enough to said tree we would realize that either one side of the tree was bare or it was three trees standing together. We usually brought home a pretty decent tree. When we would get home Dad would make a few modifications to it by drilling holes in the trunk and adding a branch here and there. My mom never liked any of the trees my dad came home with. One year, and I remember this vividly, a divorce almost occurred because my mom went and bought a tree! *GASP*... You cannot buy a tree when you come from a sawmill-owning family. It's just forbidden!

Anyway, the tree hunt was always fun. My brother, myself and Dad would make a day of it. We would play in the snow and get our clothing completely soaked. Sometimes we would stop at the sawmill and have a wiener roast. The dogs would join us on our trip as well. It was funny to see them jumping like bunnies in the deep, deep snow. Those were the days.

Then, there was the night of our elementary school Christmas concerts. That night was always magic to me. Christmas songs and Christmas plays were enjoyed and it was a great start to the holiday season. Of course the best part of the concert was waiting for Santa to arrive. He always came at the end jingling his bells. Those few moments that you got to sit on Santa's lap to tell him what you had secretly wished for, for Christmas, were pure happiness. And then there was the bag of treats he gave us. The treats were nothing special. Each of us received a little brown paper bag full of peanuts, maybe a few candies, a mandarin orange and a candy cane. We loved them though and looked forward every year to getting our sweet little treat bag.

My most favourite Christmas tradition growing up though was going to Midnight Mass, followed by a big family gathering at my grandma and grandpa's. We would get all dressed up for Midnight Mass and head to the church. The church was, or is, practically in our back yard. The church would always be beautifully decorated with a tree, which sometimes I, along with a few others, would help put up; a nativity scene that I absolutely adored; and of course the Advent Wreath. Every Sunday of Advent, I looked forward to each candle being lit. I don't know why. I just did. The church back home is small. It maybe has eight pews on each side. Every Christmas all of the pews would be full and people would place chairs in the aisles to accommodate the bigger crowd. A lot of people had to stand as well and I remember sometimes that the back porch would even be full.

After Midnight Mass we would head down the street to Grandma and Grandpa's for a feast and family gathering. When we were older we would walk there. It was awesome walking in the crisp winter air. We didn't care how cold it was, we were too excited to celebrate with everyone. The food was always top-notch. Grandma, my aunts and my mom sure knew how to cook! And then there were the Christmas crackers! How can I forget those? I was always scared to hear and feel the pop. But it was a great tradition to tear those suckers apart! And we all enjoyed being king or queen for the evening with our fancy paper crowns gracing the tops of our little noggins.

We would end up staying at Grandma and Grandpa's until the wee hours of the morning. Afterwards, we would head back home, get our cookies and milk ready for Santa, and head to bed. We barely got any sleep that night. And we always managed to be up around 5:30–6:00 a.m. to open presents. Mom and Dad rarely complained though. I think they were secretly just as excited as we were.

A few years later, when I got older, Midnight Mass was held earlier in the evening. I am not sure why the change was necessary but we rolled with it. Before church, we would have a big family feast at our little house (sometimes both sides of the family) and then we would all make our way to Mass.

Christmas Day was spent with family. After opening presents we would call everyone and wish them a Merry Christmas. In the afternoon we would either go visit with our cousins or they would come over to see what presents we received. Then, there would be another big family feast to share with one another.

It makes me sad that my boys won't grow up with the same traditions I did.

I do plan on taking them to Christmas Mass but most likely on Christmas morning. My husband isn't too thrilled with this idea. He's not really a churchgoer (and I don't go regularly myself but hope to go more in the following year). But I do want my boys to know the true meaning of Christmas.

We also do not going out hunting for a tree. I don't trust hubby with a hammer, never mind a chainsaw! We have an artificial tree. We just bought a new one on Boxing Day last year. It actually looks like a real tree. Instead of paper needles it has plastic needles that look really life-like. Maybe when the boys are older we will go out tree hunting.

Then, there is hubby's work schedule. He works shift work and therefore, sometimes has to work during Christmas. Plus, my dad and stepmom spend every second Christmas away in the city with my stepmom's family.

I was trying to think of some new traditions for our little family. After church on Christmas Day I am going to make waffles (my grandma's recipe) and serve it to the boy's with vanilla ice cream and maple syrup. That is another favourite memory shared with my grandparents whenever we slept over and I hope to make it a Christmas morning tradition for years to come. For Christmas supper we are thinking of having a roasted, stuffed chicken along with mashed potatoes and vegetables.

I did start the Book Advent Calendar with the boys and its been going very well. Sometimes life gets in the way and we forget a book or two (or four) but we are catching up. I love when my oldest says it is time for "family book time."

Top: Hochheim Christmas 1988: "Take #7 and the only person ready is the camera guy lounging in front." Bottom: family Christmas card (2006). Photo credit: Martha Hochheim.

Christmas at the Hochheims'

Martha Hochheim
Winnipeg, 1980s–90s

Martha Hochheim recalls her family's German Mennonite traditions at Christmas. Her husband, Klaus, was my friend and colleague, who lost his life in an accident in the Canadian Arctic in 2013. I am honoured to present their family's story here.

CHRISTMAS WAS ALWAYS A very special time in the Hochheim family. Klaus's mom had the cookie containers filled well before the beginning of the Advent season with a variety of German spice cookies. The smells and scents were hard to resist. First Advent was the beginning of the festivities and she was ready! Sunday evening she prepared the table elaborately, including a centre Advent wreath of pine branches that held the precious baked goodies. With individual candles lit at each place setting, this created a lovely scene. One Christmas I burnt a hole in the sleeve of my blouse as I reached over the candle for the cookie that was enticing me—ouch!

I loved adopting the German traditions around the Christmas season. About three weeks before Christmas was *Nikolaustag*. In Germany, children everywhere write their Christmas wish list on a note, place it into a shoe which is then placed outside the bedroom door overnight for St. Nikolaus to retrieve. In the morning, the good kids wake up to find a variety of candies and cookies in their shoe and the note is gone and the bad children wake up to find a shoe with a stick, known in German as a *rute*. For me, this was such a wonderfully magical experience that I didn't want our kids to miss out on, so we embraced it, always filling our children's shoes with peanuts, chocolate and cookies. As the kids got older and didn't really believe in Santa anymore, the letters changed from being addressed "Dear Nikolaus" to "Dear Santa *Klaus*." A little play on words kept the fun going until the kids were in high school!

Every Christmas we would take family photos with Opa behind the lens. This was always an adventure as it involved a tripod and trying to get everyone looking at the camera. Success was not always achieved due to the distraction of Opa throwing himself in front, laying "model style" on the carpet. One year we decided to take our own family picture and send it as a card to family and friends; the photo Christmas card as seen here (opposite page).

Lighting of City Hall Christmas Tree in Flin Flon, 1993. Photo courtesy of The Reminder (Flin Flon) *and the Flin Flon Heritage Project.*

Crossing the Chief Peguis

Jennifer Collerone
Winnipeg, 1990s–2000s

The fondest Christmas memories are sometimes the simplest ones. Jennifer Collerone reminiscences about her childhood trips to her great-aunt's home on Christmas Eve and the excitement of crossing a particular bridge on the way there.

WHEN I WAS YOUNG and the holidays came, time stretched out until I thought it had screeched to a jarring halt. Waiting for Christmas turned into an impatient blur, with periods of rushing about and wondering if Santa would rather have chocolate chip cookies or ginger snaps, how many carrots reindeer ate, and staring at a large glass of eggnog until my mom told me it'd go warm before Santa came. That resulted in a stomach ache, because of course I had to drink the eggnog instead of putting it back in the fridge.

But when darkness finally fell on Christmas Eve, I knew that all my impatient waiting had finally paid off. Santa was coming. Not in a week. Not in a couple days. That. Night. Traditionally my parents, my sister, and I would pack up into the family van and head towards my great-aunt's house in North Kildonan. Which meant going over the Chief Peguis Bridge, the coolest of all Winnipeg bridges, in my younger self's all-knowing opinion.

Every year my sister and I would watch, noses pressed to the frosted windows, for the apartment buildings that would loom up beyond the road as we passed over the river. The balconies of the buildings would be laced with lights. Some with simple strings in a single colour, others with a mish-mash of patterns so complicated, it was hard to figure out how many strands they used. And every Christmas Eve, my sister and I would hope that this was the magical year that all the balconies would have lights.

One year, only a few balconies were unlit. A new record. We were so proud, though it had nothing to do with us. Christmas Eve dinner was particularly special that year. My great-aunt prepared an amazing feast, as usual, featuring many of the traditional Ukrainian foods her mother made during the holidays. And while I was never a fan of head cheese after I found out it wasn't actually cheese, nor was it Jell-O, the perogies and perishky were always favourites.

Manitoba at Christmas

As the years passed, we never did see all the balconies lit. And when my great-aunt passed away from her battle with cancer, we were all a little lost on Christmas Eve. Our family tried a couple of different events to try and fill the gap in our holiday celebrations. One year we started spending the evening eating dinner with family friends. It became our new tradition. And that brought us over the Chief Peguis once again.

My sister and I are no longer children, but every year we still look for the apartment building balconies over the bridge and wonder if they'll all be lit up. It reminds me of my great-aunt. Her amazing food. And the happy memories we had around her table. While she is no longer with us, she is still part of our Christmas Eve.

Crossing the Chief Peguis (Kildonan Settlers) Bridge.

On the Doorstep

Sheila McKay
R.M. of Cartier, 2000s

The final tale of this anthology is courtesy of hairstylist Sheila McKay, who told me the story while snipping away at my hair. It has the honour of being the first story that I collected for this anthology, and it also illustrates the simple magic that parents try to create for their kids during the holidays. Sheila begged off from writing the story herself, so I have taken the liberty of writing it for her, with her approval.

Each Christmas, Sheila and her son Brady head out to her parents' home in Cartier, which is west of Winnipeg, near St. François Xavier. In Cartier, they are usually joined by Sheila's brother, Blaine, and occasionally by other family members.

Brady's grandma has baked up storm by then, and peanut butter & marshmallow squares, shortbread, and Stir-Me-Nots await their arrival.

On Christmas Eve, Sheila's brother excuses himself and secretly heads to the garage. Once there, he jingles some bells loudly enough to be heard in the house. Playing along, Sheila will run to the window and shout, "Oh my God, Brady! Look, I see Santa!" But by the time little Brady gets to the window, Santa has conveniently disappeared from view.

Continuing with her Oscar-worthy performance, Sheila would then claim to hear something at the door. "Wait, what's that? I think I heard something at the door, Brady! Let's go and see!" And sure enough, once they opened the door, there was a neatly wrapped present for Brady on the doorstep.

I asked Sheila if Brady has ever wondered why Santa doesn't slide down the chimney, the way he's supposed to. She has it covered, she said. She tells Brady that Santa has two ways of leaving gifts: down the chimney and on the doorstep. Plus, they usually have a roaring fire going in the fireplace, Sheila explained, so Santa couldn't possibly come down that way!

Eat and Be Merry: Holiday Recipes in Manitoba

Christmas Dinner

IN THE GRILL

Earle Hill will provide a program of ensemble music between the hours of 12.15 and 2.15.

Hors D'Oeuvres
Fruit Cocktail Poinsetta
Old English Beef Broth or Cream of Tomato
Roast Young Turkey with Chestnut Stuffing
and Cranberry Sauce   or
Fried Baby Bear Steak, Red Currant Jelly
or
Baked Suckling Pig with Apple Sauce
Mashed Turnips   Giant Green Peas
Christmas Tree Salad
Old English Plum Pudding with Hard Sauce
Hot Mince Pie   Apple Pie with Whipped Cream
Rolls and Butter   Tea or Coffee
After-Dinner Mints

$1.00

Grill Room, Fifth Floor, Donald

The Spanish Coffee Court

Will Serve a Turkey Christmas Dinner

Iced Celery and Olives
Oysters on the Half Shell
Old-Fashioned Beef Broth
Roast Young Turkey—Chestnut Stuffing—Cranberry Jelly
Boiled Creamy Mashed or Candied Sweet Potatoes
Green Peas
Christmas Tree Salad
Individual Deep Apple Pie a la Mode or Whipped Cream
Hot Mince Pie
Homemade Plum Pudding with Hard Sauce
Ice Cream with Christmas Cake
After-Dinner Mints
Rolls and Muffins   Tea or Coffee

$1.00

Spanish Coffee Court, Seventh Floor, South

Christmas dinner menu at Eaton's, downtown Winnipeg (1930).

Holiday Recipes

Eaton's Dark Fruitcake

According to Bruce Kopytek, author of Eaton's The Trans-Canada Store, *"Eaton's food departments produced a famously rich dark fruitcake that became a holiday standard from coast to coast in Canada." This recipe for Eaton's renowned fruitcake comes from* Lunch with Lady Eaton: Inside the Dining Rooms of a Nation *by Carol Anderson and Katherine Mallinson, and is reprinted courtesy of ECW Press.*

Ingredients

- 1 lb butter
- 1 lb granulated sugar
- 8 eggs
- 2 lb raisins
- 2 lb currants
- 1 lb mixed candied peel, chopped
- ½ lb almonds
- 1½ lb dates, chopped
- ½ lb glazed red and green cherries
- ¾ tbsp. cinnamon
- ¾ tbsp. nutmeg
- ¾ tbsp. cloves
- 1 lb all-purpose flour
- ½ tsp. baking soda
- ½ lemon, both juice and rind
- ½ cup grape or pineapple juice

Method

1. Prepare fruit by washing raisins and currants. Cut cherries in half; blanch almonds and split in half.

2. Dry washed fruit thoroughly and mix fruit, nuts and peel with part of the flour, so that each piece is separate and coated with flour.

3. Cream butter; add sugar gradually, beating well after each addition. Beat eggs and add.

4. Sift remaining flour with spices and soda into butter mixture, adding alternately with fruit juice.

5. Stir in fruit and mix until completely blended.

6. Pour into prepared cake pans lined with 3 layers of brown paper with a top layer of greased wax paper.

7. Bake at 250°F for approximately 3 hours, or until cake is firm and no longer sizzles when pressed lightly with fingertip. Cool on cake rack until thoroughly cooled. Wrap in foil and store in a cake tin.

Makes 2 large cakes, or 1 large cake and 12 small gift-sized loaves.

To this recipe may be added any or all of the following:

- ⅛ lb glazed pineapple
- ⅛ lb candied ginger
- ½ cup grape jelly
- 1 oz. melted chocolate

Holiday Recipes

CNR Plum Pudding

This next recipe pays homage to the importance of the railway in Manitoba's history. This classic plum pudding was served on CN passenger trains for many decades. At its peak popularity, CN served several tons of this pudding during the holiday season. It was introduced to the railway in the late 1930s by Joseph Nellis, CN's dining car chef instructor. It proved to be so popular that it was also produced and sold in a canned version.

Ingredients

- ½ lb bread crumbs
- ½ lb beef suet
- 2 oz. flour
- ½ lb brown sugar
- 2 oz. mixed peel
- pinch salt
- ¼ tsp. baking soda
- grated rind and juice of half a lemon
- ¼ pint milk
- 3 eggs
- ¼ lb sultanas
- ¼ lb raisins
- ¼ lb currants
- ¼ oz. cinnamon
- ¼ oz. nutmeg
- ¼ oz. allspice
- 1-½ oz. brandy

Method

1. Mix the ingredients together thoroughly, then add the beaten eggs, milk and brandy, and mix all together thoroughly.
2. Grease inside of pudding bowl or covered mold to prevent pudding from sticking. If pudding bowl used, cover bowl with floured gauze tied tightly around bowl to keep moisture away from pudding.
3. Boil pudding for three hours.
4. Heat thoroughly before serving, then unmold from dish. Serve with sprig of holly on top.

Makes 2-½ pounds, ten generous individual portions.

If it is desired to serve brandy with pudding, unmold plum pudding on dish, place sprig of holly on top of pudding, pour brandy around base, light brandy with match. Serve with hard sauce.

Vinarterta

Vinarterta is a traditional Icelandic fruitcake that is a holiday staple for many Manitobans of Icelandic descent. The following recipe comes from Black Currants & Caribou, *the third cookbook in the* Blueberries & Polar Bears *cookbook series by Helen Webber and Marie Woolsey. The recipe was handed down for generations in Helen's Icelandic family, and is served only on festive occasions. The recipe is reprinted courtesy of Shari Wright and Webber's Lodges, a Manitoban outfitter.*

Ingredients

Shortbread (6 layers)

- 1 cup (250 ml) butter (no substitute)
- 1-½ cups (375 ml) white sugar
- 2 eggs
- 2 tbsp. (30 ml) cream OR evaporated milk
- 1 tbsp. (15 ml) almond extract
- 4 cups (1 L) flour
- 1 tsp. (5 ml) baking powder
- 1 tsp. (5 ml) ground cardamom seed

Prune Filling

- 12 oz. (340 g) pkg. pitted prunes
- ½ cup (125 ml) water in which prunes have been boiled
- 1 cup (250 ml) white sugar
- 1 tbsp. (15 ml) cinnamon
- 1 tsp. (5 ml) vanilla

Butter Icing

- ¼ cup (60 ml) butter
- 2 cups (500 ml) icing sugar
- 1–2 tbsp. (15–30 ml) milk
- 1 tsp. (5 ml) almond extract

Method

1. To make the shortbread layers, cream together the butter and sugar. Add the eggs one at a time, beating well each time. Add cream and almond extract and beat well.

2. Sift together flour, baking powder and ground cardamom and add to creamed mixture a little at a time. You will need to knead the flour into the mixture. (A dough hook is a great boon in today's kitchen.)

3. Divide the dough into six equal parts.

4. Line a 9-in. (23 cm) square baking pan with foil. Pat one part of the dough into the pan. Remove foil with dough, and place on a cookie sheet. Repeat five times. Bake the final piece of dough in the cake pan.

5. Bake the shortbread at 375°F (190°C) for 10–12 minutes, until just lightly browned on the edges. Turn over carefully onto a cooling rack; let cool with the foil on for a couple of minutes, then remove the foil and let cool completely.

6. To make the filling, cover the prunes with water and boil until soft. Add more water if necessary during cooking. Drain, reserving ½ cup (125 ml) of water.

7. Put prunes and ½ (125 ml) cup of water in a blender and process until smooth. (Helen's grandmother never had it so easy!) A hand blender also works well.

8. Add sugar, cinnamon and vanilla to puréed prunes in a saucepan and bring to a boil. Let cool.

9. Layer cooled shortbread with cooled prune filling, beginning and ending with a shortbread layer.

10. To make the butter icing, mix together all the ingredients until creamy. If the icing is too stiff to spread, add a bit more milk, 1 tsp. (5 ml) at a time. This icing should be a bit on the stiff side.

11. Ice the top of the cake.

12. Wrap the cake in foil or plastic wrap and keep it airtight for 3–4 days. This gives the shortbread layers a chance to soften up.

    Makes 72 slices.

Serving suggestion: Slice ½-in. (1.3 cm) slices and cut each slice in 2-in. (5 cm) pieces. (Cut in small pieces like a fruitcake.)

Note: This will keep for a month in a cool place. It freezes well for longer storage.

Plumi Moos

Margaret Fast presents a traditional Mennonite recipe for Plumi Moos, *a kind of fruit soup often served at holiday meals. Although it can be served on any occasion, in Margaret's family it was made only at Christmas.*

Ingredients

- 2 quarts water
- 1 cup raisins
- 1 cup prunes
- ¼ cup dried apricots
- ½ cup sugar
- 6 tbsp. flour
- ½ tsp. salt

Method

1. In a large pot bring water to a boil and add the fruit.
2. Simmer until fruit is tender.
3. Prepare paste with flour, sugar and salt. Slowly add flour paste to the fruit mixture, stirring constantly.
4. Cook until slightly thickened.

Serve warm or cold.

Holiday Recipes

Ukrainian Christmas Eve Holubtsi (Cabbage Rolls)

Petrosha shares her recipe for Holubtsi, *one of the traditional dishes served on* Sviat Vechir *(Christmas Eve) in Ukrainian homes. More recipes can be found on her blog, petroshasblog.wordpress.com.*

Ingredients

- 1 large head green cabbage
- 2 cups white rice
- 4 cups water
- ¼ cup vinegar
- 1 large onion (chopped fine)
- 1 tsp. salt and pepper (or to taste)
- 1 20 oz. can tomato soup plus one can of water

Method

1. Remove the core from the cabbage and place in a large pot of boiling water with vinegar and salt added.
2. Loosen the outer leaves one at a time and remove from the water when soft and wilted, but not cooked.
3. Cool under cold water and cut away the middle core of each leaf, and cut the cabbage leaves slightly smaller than the palm of your hand.
4. Now rinse the rice several times to remove surface starch.
5. Put the rice in a pot, add salt and 4 cups water.
6. Cover with a tight-fitting lid, and bring to a boil.
7. Turn off the stove and leave for 30 minutes. Do not take off the lid.
8. In the meantime, fry the onions in the vegetable oil until soft. If these are NOT for Christmas Eve, you can finely chop and fry bacon with the onions.
9. When the rice is cooked, add half of the onions and mix well. Line a roaster with foil and then any extra-large cabbage leaves.

10. Place about 1 tablespoon of rice in each leaf and roll tightly. Place side by side (one layer) in the prepared roaster. Pour some of the tomato soup mixture and some of the onions on every layer. When the roaster is full, pour the remaining tomato soup mixture on the top. Cover with foil.

11. Bake at 300°F for about 2-½ hours or until the cabbage is tender. To test if done, stick a fork through the cabbage rolls. The cabbage should be soft and fork tender.

Note: Option to steaming off the cabbage leaves—core the cabbage and place it as a whole head into your freezer. When ready to make holubtsi, defrost. The leaves will be soft and pliable. Rinse under cold water, cut the leaves in half and take any of the coarse ribs off.

Pfeffernüsse

Grace Warkentin provides her family's recipe for Pfeffernüsse, a German spice cookie. "Our mother would bake these well ahead of Christmas and store them in a clean pillow case, and hang them from the upstairs rafters, or they would be eaten way before Christmas. They were a refreshing homemade treat that we tossed into our mouths like peanuts. Our dad liked to dip them into his breakfast coffee. Yum!"

Ingredients

- 2 cups sugar
- 1-½ cup shortening
- 1 cup syrup or honey
- ⅓ cup buttermilk
- 2 eggs
- 1 tsp. baking soda
- ½ tsp. salt
- 1 tsp. nutmeg
- 1 tsp. ginger
- 1 tsp. cinnamon
- 1 tsp. anise seed
- 1 tsp. cardamom
- about 6 cups flour or a bit more to make a soft dough

Method

1. Preheat oven to 350°F.
2. In a large bowl, cream together shortening, sugar, syrup or honey, buttermilk, and eggs.
3. Combine all the spices and the baking powder and baking soda and stir into creamed mixture.

4. Add flour a cup at a time until mixture becomes a soft, pliable dough.

5. Chill dough in fridge overnight or for at least a few hours.

6. Sprinkle flour on countertop and take a fairly large chunk of dough and roll into a long ¾-inch diameter rope. Continue to do this until all the dough is rolled out.

7. Place the ropes on large ungreased cookie sheets and chill again. This will make for easier cutting.

8. Slice ropes into ½-inch bite-sized pieces.

9. Place pieces on ungreased cookie sheets.

10. Bake at 350°F for 6–8 minutes. Remove from oven and place on cooling racks.

11. When cool, store in cookie tins. They will last for several months.

These are buttery, crispy morsels, and the delicate flavour of anise and cardamom enhance the taste.

Holiday Recipes

Slovak Kapustnica and Bobalky

The next set of recipes is from Mark Vajcner in Regina. "Here is a Slovak Christmas Eve dinner that I remember from growing up in Winnipeg in the 1970s and 1980s. These are traditional dishes from the eastern regions of Slovakia and their origins probably go back centuries. It was customary to have Kapustnica and Bobalky every Christmas and New Year."

Kapustnica (Sauerkraut and Sausage Soup)

Ingredients

- ½ lb smoked pork or ham—ham hocks work best
- 5 cups water
- ⅛ tsp. black pepper
- ½ tsp. salt
- 1 bay leaf
- 1 small onion, sliced thinly
- 1 tbsp. oil
- 2 tsp. Hungarian paprika powder
- 1 cup sauerkraut
- 2 oz. mushrooms, sliced
- 1 clove garlic, minced
- 1 Hungarian or Polish-style smoked sausage (250 g)
- ½ tsp. caraway seeds (optional)
- ½ tsp. sugar
- ½ tbsp. white vinegar

Method

1. In a large dutch oven, combine smoked ham, water, black pepper, salt, and bay leaf. Bring to a boil, cover and simmer at a lower heat for 30 minutes.

2. Meanwhile, slice and sauté onion in oil in a separate frying pan. Onions should be translucent but not brown. Now add paprika powder and stir well into the onions. Remove from heat.

3. Drain the sauerkraut and add to the dutch oven after the initial 30 minutes are up. Stir in the sautéed onions, mushrooms, and garlic. Cover and simmer for another 30 minutes.

4. Now remove ham from the soup and cut meat away from bone and skin. Chop meat into pieces and return to the soup. Cut up sausage and add to the soup along with caraway seeds, sugar, and vinegar.

5. Cover and simmer a final 15 minutes.

6. Serve with a dollop of sour cream.

Bobalky (Bread Dumplings)

"The Bobalky I remember were always made with fresh bread dough, but today, one can use frozen bread roll dough from the supermarket. Either prepare or buy about one pound of bread dough."

Ingredients

- 1 lb bread dough (fresh or frozen)
- 750 g dry curd cottage cheese
- 2 tbsp. butter

Method

1. Pinch off portions of bread dough into small pieces about half an inch in diameter.

2. Place on a greased cookie sheet, set in a warm location, and let rise for about 15 minutes. Note, some of the bread pieces will probably now be touching each other. This is okay.

Holiday Recipes

3. Bake at 375°F for 15 to 20 minutes or until lightly browned.

4. When cool, break the bread into pieces. Bobalky can be prepared beforehand and stored in a cool and dry place until needed.

5. Typically Bobalky are topped with poppy seeds but we ate them topped with cottage cheese. In a large mixing bowl place 750 grams of dry curd cottage cheese. Mash the curds with a potato masher for a finer consistency and set aside.

6. In a saucepan melt 2 tbsp. of butter, being careful not to burn or brown it.

7. The Bobalky now need to be prepared. To soften them up, pour boiling water over the Bobalky in a colander. Be careful not to make them too mushy. They are best when still a little crunchy.

8. Drain the Bobalky well and then pour into the cottage cheese.

9. Now pour the melted butter evenly over the Bobalky and mix well with a large spoon.

10. Add salt and pepper to taste.

Winnipeg realtor Crystal LeGoff provides the next two recipes, which are staples at her family's Christmas dinners.

Broccoli Casserole

I had never heard of anyone serving broccoli casserole for Christmas dinner, but after researching it online, I discovered that it wasn't too unusual as a holiday dish. When I mentioned this to Crystal, she said, "Good to know others have broccoli casserole at Christmas too! I thought maybe it was just our family. It has been a tradition in our family for years."

Ingredients

- ½ lb cheddar cheese (grated)
- 2 lb broccoli (fresh or frozen)
- 1 pkg. Uncle Ben's Classics Wild Rice
- 1 can cream of mushroom soup
- 1 can cream of broccoli soup

Method

1. Cook rice as per package directions.
2. Cook broccoli until softened.
3. Mix together soup and cheese.
4. Butter casserole dish.
5. Layer rice, broccoli, and cheese mixture.
6. Top with extra cheddar (optional).
7. Bake at 350°F for approximately 1 hour (until bubbly and warm).

Grandma's Shortbread

When I asked Crystal why her shortbread is baked on an upside-down cookie sheet, she said she had no idea and her grandmother was no longer around to ask. "I asked my mom, and she thought it was to help the cookies brown on the sides but was not really sure. I don't think it matters that much."

For the paper lining the cookie sheets, "I use a brown paper grocer bag and cut it to fit the tray, I have also used a couple of the brown paper lunch bags in a pinch. The brown paper is used because there is a lot of butter in the mixture. It absorbs the grease and gives the bottom of the shortbread a nice golden colour. I have tried using parchment paper and it can work but the cookies came out a bit soft on the bottom with that method."

Ingredients

- 1 lb butter
- 4 cups flour
- 1 cup brown sugar
- 2 tbsp. corn starch

Method

1. Cream butter and brown sugar and mix well. Gradually add flour and corn starch.
2. Roll out dough and cut with cookie cutter.
3. Bake at 250°F for 1 hour (place on upside-down cookie sheet covered with brown paper). Makes approximately 12–15 cookies.

Christmas Sweets: Delectable Gifts That the Kitchen May Provide

Grain Growers' Guide, December 9, 1914

Christmas just isn't Christmas without some sweet treats to snack on. In 1914, the Grain Growers' Guide *published these recipes for popcorn balls and other candied treats. The recipes are reprinted courtesy of Farm Business Communications.*

Corn Balls are always a favourite with children, and may be made easily during the crisp days of winter. If wrapped in squares of paraffin paper they are acceptable Christmas tree ornaments, especially if provided with the ribbon upon which are the words "Merry Christmas." If one does not print well, the little letters made from macaroni (the kind that are seen frequently in soups), or celluloid letters, may be glued on. A basket trimmed with holly shows corn balls to advantage. Recipes for molasses and sugar corn balls are given.

Popped Corn Balls No. I.—Pop corn, pick over (discarding kernels that have not popped), and put in large kettle; there should be three quarts. Sprinkle with one-half teaspoon of salt. Melt one tablespoonful of butter in saucepan and add one cupful of molasses and one-half cupful of sugar. Bring to the boiling point and let boil until mixture will become brittle when tried in cold water. Pour mixture gradually, while stirring constantly, over corn, turning the corn frequently that the kernels may be well coated. Shape into balls using as little pressure as possible.

Corn Balls No. II.—Pop corn, pick over, and put in a large kettle; there should be five quarts. Put two cupfuls of sugar, one-half cupful of white syrup, one-third teaspoonful of salt, and one and one-half cupfuls of water in saucepan. Bring to the boiling point, and let boil without stirring until thermometer registers 260 degrees F. Add one teaspoonful of vinegar and one tablespoonful of vanilla, and continue the boiling until thermometer reaches 264 degrees F. Remove from range and pour over corn gradually, while stirring constantly. Make into balls, using as little pressure as possible. Wintergreen flavouring may be used in place of vanilla.

A homemade **French Nougat** has a very professional look if you but follow the rule carefully. Put one-half pound confectioner's (not powdered) sugar in a saucepan, place on range and stir constantly until melted; then add one-fourth pound of Jordan almonds, blanched and finely chopped. Pour on a slightly oiled marble slab. As mixture spreads fold toward centre, using a broad-bladed knife, keeping mixture constantly in motion. Divide into four parts, and as soon as cool enough to handle shape in long rolls, about one-third inch in diameter, keeping well in motion, until almost cold. When cold snap in pieces one and one-half inches long. This is accomplished by holding roll at point to be snapped over the sharp edge of a broad-bladed knife, and snapping. Melt confectioner's dipping chocolate in a small saucepan placed in a larger saucepan, containing boiling water, and beat with a fork two minutes. Dip pieces separately in chocolate and with a two-tined fork or bon-bon dipper remove to oiled paper or paraffin paper, drawing dipper through top of each the entire length thus leaving a ridge of the chocolate on top.

Fruit Paste, if packed in layers in a Christmas box or basket, makes an appropriate gift well suited to the palate of the average man. When packing, put a piece of paraffin paper between each two layers. Pick over and remove stones from one pound of dates. Mix fruit with one-half pound each, filberts and English walnut meats, and force through a meat chopper. Work, using the hands, on a board dredged with confectioner's sugar, until well blended. Pat and roll to one-fourth inch in thickness, using confectioner's sugar for dredging board and pin. Shape with a small, round cutter, first dipped in sugar, or cut in three-fourths-inch squares, using a sharp knife. Roll each piece in confectioner's sugar, and shake to remove superfluous sugar.

It is well to have for the Christmas spread a large ornamented Cake which will do well for the children as for the grown-ups. Here is a description of just such a one, in which pound cake and lady fingers recipes were used. It makes a very attractive centrepiece for the table when finished. The top and sides of the large cake were covered with confectioner's frosting, and the words "Merry Christmas" cut from angelica, first softened in warm water, were placed; then little, hard round red candies and halves of pistachio nuts were added for extra garnish. The lady fingers were arranged, pressed slightly into the frosting, and tied with a red ribbon, while a small bunch of holly completed the decoration.

Pound Cakes.—Work one and three-fourths cupfuls of butter until creamy, and add three cupfuls of flour (pastry, once sifted) gradually, while beating constantly. Beat the yolks of ten eggs until thick and lemon-coloured, and add three cupfuls of powdered sugar gradually, while beating constantly. Combine mixtures, add whites of ten eggs, beaten until stiff, and sift over two teaspoonfuls of baking powder. Beat vigorously and turn into a buttered and floured round tin. Bake in a moderate oven (350°F) one and one-half hours.

Fruit Fudge.—Boil three cupfuls of granulated sugar, three teaspoonfuls of cocoa, three-quarters of a cupful of milk and one tablespoon of butter. When it will form a soft ball in cold water, add one-half cupful each of chopped raisins and nuts, one-quarter of a cupful of coconut and three-quarters of a cupful of figs, cut in small pieces. Pour into a buttered pan and when partly cool, mark into squares.

Peanut Fudge.—Boil three cupfuls of brown sugar with one cupful of milk until a soft ball can be formed in cold water; take from the fire, add two tablespoonfuls of peanut butter and beat until creamy. Pour into a buttered pan and mark in squares when cool.

Nan and Auntie Brenda's Guyanese Fruitcake

Claire Herbert sends in this recipe for Guyanese Fruitcake, which is usually made at Christmas and for weddings. She also relates an intriguing use for them: "In Guyana, like many Caribbean countries, slaves were brought from Africa, where gold bangles were worn by women to show the prosperity of their families. They were also used for trading if the families were very prosperous. These bracelets were passed down from mother to daughter.

"My mum moved to England from Guyana when she was 11. My great grandmother baked the gold bracelet for my mum into the Guyanese fruitcake and posted it to England because she didn't trust the postal service not to take the gold, and also because it had once been a crime for any non-white person to own gold in Guyana. When I was living in Brandon, my mum gave me the bracelet I now have. It didn't arrive in a fruitcake, though!"

Ingredients

- 2 tins Mackeson Stout (330 ml each). This is a milk stout containing lactose. In Canada, Young's Double Chocolate Stout may be more readily available. If using Young's Stout, 1 bottle (500 ml) is enough.
- 1 lb soft brown sugar
- 1 lb currants
- 1 lb raisins
- large packet of peeled almonds
- 1 lb prunes
- at least ¾ bottle (26 oz.) of Ruby Port
- 12 eggs
- approximately 1 cup flour, self-raising
- ½ lb butter
- ½ lb margarine
- vanilla essence to taste (~¼ tbsp.)
- about 2 tsp. baking powder (or ~4 tsp. if not using self-raising flour)
- rum
- 3 regular size baking tins with removable sides (e.g., springform pan)
- 1 small baking tin (for a "test" cake)
- 4L jar with lid

Method

Set Fruit (the longer the better, at least one month)

1. Grind fruit in food processor until coarsely ground.

Holiday Recipes

2. Put fruit into jar.
3. Melt sugar on low heat. Keep stirring so sugar does not crystallize. When almost melted, add in stout (be careful as it will bubble up).
4. Leave overnight until cold.
5. Pour stout into jar and mix with wooden spoon until it is well blended with the fruit.
6. Pour port on top.
7. Wait until port settles, then pour some rum.
8. Leave marinating in jar until baking day.

To Bake

1. Grease cake tins and line with parchment paper so that paper extends over sides of pan.
2. Beat eggs in a bowl.
3. In a separate bowl, cream butter and margarine. Add brown sugar and mix well.
4. Add eggs to mixture.
5. Add fruit and mix well.
6. Stir in flour and baking powder, bit by bit (about ¼ cup flour at a time) and test after each time until a wooden spoon can stand upright in the mixture (can lean slowly to side).
7. Fill tins about ¾ full.
8. Bake at gas mark 4 (350°F).
9. Test for doneness by putting a knife into the centre of the cake. When knife comes out clean, cake is done. Tip: Run knife under cold water before testing in cake.
10. After cake has cooled, poke small holes in cake and pour port on top until cake is saturated. Cover cake.
11. Every few days continue to pour port over cake to keep moist, until time to serve.

Stir-Me-Nots

Sheila McKay contributes a recipe for the delicious Stir-Me-Not squares mentioned in her story, "On the Doorstep."

Ingredients

- 1 stick (½ cup) butter
- 1-½ cups graham cracker crumbs
- 3-½ oz. shredded coconut
- ½ cup butterscotch chips
- 1 pkg. (12 oz.) chocolate chips
- 1 can (300 ml) condensed milk
- 1 cup walnuts, chopped

Method

1. Preheat oven to 350°F.
2. Melt butter and pour into 9" x 13" glass baking pan.
3. Evenly layer the graham cracker crumbs, followed by the coconut, chocolate chips, and butterscotch chips.
4. Pour condensed milk over the layers.
5. Top with chopped walnuts.
6. Bake 350°F for 30–35 minutes.
7. Let cool for at least 10 minutes before cutting into squares.

Filipino-Style Grilled Pork Skewers

Barbecued meat is a staple at Filipino gatherings. Kristine Tubiera provides her recipe for grilled pork skewers. She suggests serving them as an appetizer, main course, or a late-night snack at your next holiday gathering.

Ingredients

- pork tenderloin
- 4 cloves of garlic
- ¼ cup soy sauce
- ¼ cup brown sugar
- ½ cup Sprite or ginger ale
- 12 bamboo skewers

Method

1. Slice pork tenderloin into pieces.
2. Make marinade by combining garlic, soy sauce, brown sugar and Sprite/ginger ale.
3. Add pork to marinade and refrigerate overnight.
4. Soak bamboo skewers for 1 hour (minimum) in water.
5. Thread marinated pork onto each skewer.
6. Boil excess marinade to use for basting.
7. Grill on barbecue for 8–10 minutes, basting occasionally.

Alexander Küchen

Melanie Reimer shares this recipe for Alexander Küchen, a type of cookie with a raspberry filling.

Ingredients

- 1 or 2 lb butter
- 5 cups flour
- ½ cup sugar
- raspberry jam (for filling)

Method

1. Use 4 cups of flour to start, blend flour, butter, and sugar together with a pastry fork.
2. Mold dough with hands until able to roll out on floured surface.
3. Roll out to ¼-inch thickness, and cut out small circles with a small flour-rimmed glass.
4. Bake at 350°F until golden brown.
5. When cool, sandwich cookies with raspberry jam.
6. Top with icing.

Stuffing

What's a Christmas dinner without stuffing? Ashley Gaden sends in her family's favourite recipe.

Ingredients

- 2-½ cups chicken broth
- 3 onions, diced
- 6 cups diced bread
- 1 tbsp. paprika
- 1 egg
- salt and pepper

Method

1. Heat half of the broth and all the onions for 10 minutes in skillet on medium heat until onions have softened.
2. In bowl, combine cooked onions, remaining broth, and the remaining ingredients.
3. Put in turkey OR alternatively, put in casserole dish at 350°F and bake 45 minutes. Serves 12.

Oatcakes

Contributor Margaret Dennis Owen provides her family's recipe for oatcakes, which were mentioned in her story, "The Home Front."

Ingredients

- 4 cups Scotch oatmeal
- 1 cup flour
- 1 tsp. salt
- 1 tsp. baking soda
- 1–¼ cups shortening
- ¼ cup brown sugar

Method

1. Mix dry ingredients in a large bowl.
2. Melt shortening and add to dry ingredients.
3. Add ½ cup of cold water.
4. Roll out on floured board and cut into 2–½ inch rounds with a cookie cutter.
5. Bake 10 minutes at 350°F.
6. Butter oatcakes and serve with cheese.

Tourtière

This meat pie is traditionally served at revéillon, *the Christmas Eve dinner held after Midnight Mass in French-Canadian culture. The recipe is courtesy of Stéphane Pichon, whose family used to own and operate Le Croissant bakery in St. Boniface.*

Ingredients

- 1lb freshly ground meat (mix beef/pork/veal)
- 1 small onion, diced very small
- ½ tsp. salt
- ½ tsp. savory
- ¼ tsp. celery seeds
- ¼ tsp. cloves
- ½ cup water
- ¼ cup bread crumbs (more if needed)
- previously prepared pie dough (either homemade or ready-made pie crusts)

Method

1. Mix ingredients together in a large pot, and bring to a boil on medium heat for 20 minutes. Stir occasionally. Verify that onion is soft and meat is cooked.
2. Add ¼ cup of bread crumbs, mix and let rest for 10 minutes until liquid is absorbed by bread crumbs. Add more bread crumbs if necessary to absorb the liquid.
3. Use pie shell (dough) and pour in the meat mixture when cool enough to do so.
4. Cover the pie with another layer of dough and leave a hole in the centre (size of a toonie) and poke small holes in the top layer of the dough.
5. Wash top layer of dough with a beaten egg; ensure it has been brushed over entire exposed dough.
6. Bake at 400°F until cooked and pie shows golden colour.

Vispipuuro (Finnish Cranberry Pudding)

Story contributor Trish Suzanne provides a recipe for Vispipuuro, a Finnish cranberry pudding or porridge dessert that has a mousse-like consistency.

Ingredients

- 1 lb fresh cranberries
- water
- ¾ cup sugar
- ½ cup Cream of Wheat, uncooked (not instant)

Method

1. Add enough water to cover cranberries and boil until the cranberries burst.
2. Strain (makes about 3 cups of juice).
3. Pour juice into a pot, add sugar and bring to a boil.
4. Add Cream of Wheat slowly, stirring constantly to avoid lumping.
5. Boil about 20 minutes.
6. Remove from stove and pour into a large bowl.
7. Beat for approximately 20 minutes at high speed with electric beater until light coloured and fluffy.
8. Serve cold with cream.

Slush Punch

All these sweets and baked goods are probably making you thirsty! Ashley Gaden provides a recipe for a refreshing slush punch to wash it all down.

Ingredients

- 1 3-oz. (small) package of strawberry Jell-O
- 2 cups white sugar
- 6 cups pineapple juice
- 1 tbsp. almond extract
- ½ cup lemon juice

Method

1. Dissolve Jell-O and sugar in 5 cups boiling water. Let cool.
2. Add pineapple juice, almond extract, and lemon juice.
3. Pour into ice cream pail and freeze.
4. Take out 5–7 hours before serving. Spoon into glasses and mix with ginger ale.

Schuten Krapflen (Deep-Fried Cottage-Cheese Pockets)

This anthology would not be complete without a contribution from the Hutterite community, who have had a long history in Manitoba. I was not able to secure a Hutterite Christmas story, but the least I can do is to present a recipe for a holiday treat from the Hutterite culture. This recipe for Schuten Krapflen (suitably sized for a colony) is from Secrets of a Hutterite Kitchen *by Mary-Ann Kirkby, who grew up on a Hutterite colony near Portage la Prairie. It is reprinted courtesy of Penguin Random House. Thanks to Mary-Ann for providing a more detailed version of the recipe. I have added the first step to clarify the making of the dough jackets.*

Ingredients

Filling

- 24 cups dry curd cottage cheese
- 6 cups eggs
- 6 cups bread crumbs
- 1 lb butter
- 3 large onions
- ¼ cup salt

Dough

- 10 cups water
- 4 eggs
- 2 tsp. salt
- flour (enough until sides of bowl come clean)

Method

1. Prepare dough and roll out on a lightly floured surface. Cut into 2" x 3" rectangles for the dough jackets.
2. Take onions (finely chopped) and sauté onions in butter.
3. When onions are lightly brown, mix into the cottage cheese, eggs, and bread crumbs, together with the butter. Mix well.
4. Spoon onto dough jackets. Pinch together edges.
5. Cook in water or steam for 10 minutes, then in fryer until golden brown at 300°F.
6. Serve with whipped or sour cream and pancake syrup. Serves 70 people.

Story Contributors

Evelina Adams (née Sinclair) was born and raised in Shoal Lake. In 1918, she began her training as a nurse at the Neepawa General Hospital, where she worked during the Spanish flu epidemic. She was also present for the second flu outbreak in the spring of 1919. She continued her nursing career in Russell and in Spy Hill Saskatchewan, before returning to Manitoba to work at the Birtle General Hospital. She married William Adams in 1922 and had four children. Evelina passed away in Neepawa in 1990, at the age of 92.

Emma Louisa Averill (née Peacey) was born in the Cotswolds Hills area of south central England in 1850. At the age of 20, she married Octavius Averill. They had four children: Isaac, Fanny, Ethel Arabella, and Pax. Hoping to secure a better future for their children, the Averill family emigrated to Canada in 1880 and settled on a homestead near Clanwilliam, Manitoba. They farmed there for twenty years, but were plagued by adversity. Their home was destroyed by fire shortly after they moved in, as was their second home a few years later. In the second fire, the family was forced to flee in the middle of the night in winter and Emma suffered severe frostbite to her feet. Tragedy struck again in 1900, when their youngest son Pax died at the age of 25 after being thrown from a horse. This proved to be too much for the family and they decided to move to British Columbia to have a fresh start. Misfortune followed them there, however, with Emma's husband dying in an accident at the age of 60. Emma died nine years later in 1915. She was 65.

Evelyn Ballantyne is the author of *The Aboriginal Alphabet for Children*. She is a member of Opaskwayak Cree Nation and resides in The Pas, Manitoba.

Robert M. Ballantyne (1825–1894) was the son of Alexander Ballantyne and Anne Randall Scott Grant. He came to Rupert's Land from Scotland in 1841 and worked for the Hudson's Bay Company for six years. After returning to Scotland, he began a prolific literary career. He wrote several popular adventure books for young people, and authored over 70 books in total. Ballantyne died in Rome, where he was seeking treatment for Ménière's disease.

Gordon Billings was born in Manitoba and lived on his family's farm near MacGregor for 15 years, earning money by raising ducks for sale. He was a student at Southend School for grades 1–9. After his family sold the farm and moved to Portage la Prairie, Gordon continued his education at Portage Collegiate, earning his way by working at a grocery store. After finishing school, Gordon joined the banking industry and worked for one employer for almost 43 years, at various branches across the Prairies. Along the way, he picked up a loving wife and three children. They retired to Calgary and now spend the winter down in the southern States and the summer exploring Canada and going on world tours.

Leah Boulet lives beside the beautiful Winnipeg River in the little French community of St. Georges, Manitoba. She has fond recollections of searching for the perfect Christmas tree with her father, a tradition she and her husband continued with their own two children, now grown and beginning to make traditions of their own. This particular Christmas tree hunt occurred in the bush across the street from her childhood home a few miles away in Pine Falls, Manitoba in 1978. She wrote about this wonderful memory many years later and presented it to her father as a special Christmas gift.

Wayne Chan is the editor of *Manitoba at Christmas*. He is an award-winning writer whose work has appeared in local and national publications. He was formerly a community correspondent for the Canstar community newspapers. He is a graduate of the University of Manitoba and resides in Winnipeg. *Manitoba at Christmas* is his second book.

Mary Louise Chown has told stories across Canada and around the world, including the Winnipeg Folk Festival, and she has taught storytelling to all ages. Every story is a teaching story and all stories are sacred. She often adds music of drum and hammered dulcimer to her stories. You may have already heard her on CBC Radio, or at the Winnipeg Folk Festival, or read her new book, *Now I Know the World is Round: Stories at the End of Life*. She lives on a farm on the beautiful Whitemouth River, where she keeps bees and laying hens and continues to tell stories.

Jennifer Collerone is a designer in Winnipeg, though her interests range from vintage item procurement to playing soccer on local teams. Her favourite Christmas movie is *Home Alone* (she's still a child at heart), her favourite carol is O Holy Night, and yes, she does put up a stocking for her dog. Her story takes place in the '90s and early 2000s in northeast Winnipeg.

Roger Currie has worked as a broadcaster and writer for more than 45 years. These days he describes himself as "semi-retired." He still does regular newscasts on CJNU, 93.7 FM in Winnipeg. He is a happily married father and grandfather. He is passionate about movies and he currently serves on the Manitoba Film Classification Board.

Story Contributors

William A. Czumer emigrated to Canada in 1903 when he was 21. He was originally from the village of Drohoyiv in Peremyshl County, Galicia. After arriving in Winnipeg, he worked briefly for the railroad before beginning his teacher's training at the Ruthenian Training School. After graduation in 1907, William taught mainly in Manitoba until he departed in 1913 to take a teaching position in Alberta. He became a vocal proponent for establishing the same type of bilingual schools found in Manitoba, but he was met with strong opposition from the Alberta government. William was subsequently removed from his teaching post and banned from teaching in the province. Unable to follow his chosen career, he turned to farming in the Smoky Lake area of Alberta. In 1938, he and his wife Lena and their five kids moved to Edmonton to seek better educational opportunities for the children. After a short time in the second-hand furniture business, William and a partner formed the Merchant's Wholesale. He retired in 1961 and passed away in 1963.

Arthur R. Devlin was born in Antler, Saskatchewan in 1908 and spent his childhood in the Asessippi area of Manitoba. He married Janet Gillespie in 1933 and had two children. Arthur served in the Royal Canadian Navy Volunteer Reserve in World War II. After the war, he farmed and ranched in the Interlake area and was active in provincial politics, running for office in the 1962 and 1966 elections. After he retired from farming, he worked for the Department of Indian Affairs and the Canadian Executive Service Organization. Arthur died in Vancouver in 1981.

Alice Didur (née Karpiak) grew up on a Manitoba farm, but moved to Ontario after marrying her husband Alex Didur in 1943. Together they raised their four children (Gladys, David, Robert and Rose Anne). She still lives in the same house in Levack that she moved into in 1950.

David Didur was born and raised in the nickel mining town of Levack in northern Ontario. Dave earned his B.Sc. and B.Ed. at the University of Toronto. His 31-year career in education consists of 14 years in the classroom and the remainder as a consultant, curriculum co-ordinator or education officer in the field of Computers in Education.

Margaret Fast was born and grew up in rural southwestern Manitoba. After completing her medical training at the University of Manitoba she worked in Vietnam for several years and also lived and worked in England and in Kenya. However, most of her career was spent practising public health in Manitoba. She also raised three incredible children and is now spending time with four delightful grandchildren. Over the course of the past few years she has learned that scientific writing does not prepare one for creative writing and is enjoying the challenge of learning a new craft.

Mabel E. Finch was born in 1887 in Carman, Manitoba to William and Caroline Finch. She was one of four girls and two boys in the family. All four girls became teachers. In the early 1900s, she taught at Central School No. 944 near Carman and later at Transcona Central School. In the late 1920s, Mabel was secretary to the provincial Minister of Mines and Natural Resources. She was a member of the United Farm Women of Manitoba and served as its president. She also served as president of the Business and Professional Women's Club of Winnipeg and was a long-standing member of the organization. Mabel passed away at the age 97 in Winnipeg.

Mary FitzGibbon was the daughter of Charles FitzGibbon and Agnes Moodie, and the granddaughter of writer Susanna Moodie. At the age of 25, she headed for the northwest as the governess for a CPR worker's children. Based on her experiences, Mary authored *A Trip to Manitoba, or Roughing on the Line* in 1880. She also published a biography of her grandfather, titled, *A Veteran of 1812: The Life of James FitzGibbon*. She died in 1915 at the age of 63.

Vera Fryer was born in Fort Alexander, Manitoba to Rev. Charles and Elsie Fryer. She had two brothers, Stanley and Leonard. Vera attended Rupert's Land College and Normal School in Winnipeg, and then received an M.A. in English and French from the University of Manitoba in 1940. She taught school in Elkhorn, Pine Falls, Gilbert Plains, Dauphin, and in Winnipeg at Glenlawn Collegiate. After she took early retirement due to health reasons, she continued to stay active by doing volunteer work for many organizations, including Dalnavert, the Winnipeg Art Gallery, Meals on Wheels, and the Winnipeg General Hospital. She was also a long-standing member of the St. James Anglican Church in Winnipeg. Vera passed away in 1999; she was 85 years old.

Rose Fyleman was an English poet and author known for her children's poems about fairies. She was born in Nottingham, England to John and Emilie Feilman in 1877. She studied singing in France and Germany and received a diploma in music from the Royal College of Music in London. In her forties, she found success as a poet, publishing her first poem about fairies in *Punch* magazine in 1917. Her poem, "Winnipeg at Christmas" was published in 1930, shortly after she visited the city. Rose passed away in 1957.

Donna Firby Gamache is a retired teacher/writer who lives with her husband, Luc, in MacGregor. She grew up north of Minnedosa, graduated from Brandon College and taught in Souris and Gladstone, and in the MacGregor-Austin area. She has three grown sons and three grandsons. She writes regularly for the *Manitoba Co-operator*, and has been widely published in various magazines and anthologies, for children and adults. She has five published books: *Return to the River* (short stories for adults); and four books for younger readers. Her most recent book is *Where the Rolling River Runs*.

Story Contributors

Verena Garrioch was born in Portage la Prairie to Rev. A. C. Garrioch and Agnes Crabb. She had a sister, Ida, and two brothers, Stanley and Harold. Verena moved with her family to Winnipeg in 1929 and began a long career as a writer for the *Winnipeg Tribune* in 1935. She passed away in 1979, at the age of 77.

George VI was the king of the United Kingdom from 1937 until his death in 1952. He was the second son of King George V and Victoria May, the Duchess of York. He received his education at the Royal Naval College at Osborne and Dartmouth, and then joined the Royal Navy. In World War I, he served on board HMS *Collingwood* and saw action at the Battle of Jutland. After the war, he attended the University of Cambridge for a year. He became the Duke of York in 1920 and married Lady Elizabeth Bowes-Lyon in 1923. They had two children, Elizabeth and Margaret. He became king after his brother's abdication in 1937. During World War II, he was an important symbolic leader to the British people. His health declined after the war and he was diagnosed with lung cancer. He passed away in 1952.

Judy Gerstel is a Toronto writer and journalist. She grew up in Winnipeg's North End and attended St. John's High School and the University of Manitoba. She spent many a Saturday afternoon walking on Portage Avenue between Eaton's and The Bay and recalls a time when women weren't allowed in the Captain's quarters in The Bay's Paddlewheel Restaurant at lunch time, and to her regret, never wondered why or challenged it as a girl.

John J. Gunn was born in 1861 near present-day Lockport. His parents were John and Emma Gunn. His father served as the MLA for St. Andrews North and his grandfather, Donald Gunn, was a member of the first legislative council of Manitoba. J. J. Gunn became a farmer and apiarist and served as president of the Western Beekeepers' Association. He married Elanor Flanagan in 1905. They had one son, but he died in infancy. J. J. Gunn died in an accident in 1907.

Salome Halldorson was born in Lundar in 1887 to Halldor Halldorsson and Kristin Palsdottir. She received a B.A. from Wesley College in Winnipeg and became a teacher after graduation. In 1936, she was the first Icelandic woman to be elected as an MLA. She passed away in Winnipeg in 1970.

Erin Hammond is a graduate of the University of Winnipeg's Theatre and Film program. She has worked as an actor, director, playwright and drama teacher for 20 years. Erin also has an education degree and teaches Performing Arts in the Winnipeg School Division. She loves to write, create and play with kids and kids at heart.

Joseph J. Hargrave was born in York Factory in 1841, the eldest son of James Hargrave and Letitia Mactavish. His father was a chief trader for the Hudson's Bay Company and his uncle, William Mactavish, was the governor of Assiniboia and Rupert's Land. J. J. Hargrave received his education at Madras College in St. Andrews, Scotland.

After completing his studies, he came to the Red River Settlement and entered service with the Hudson's Bay Company. He began a career in journalism by writing for the *Montreal Herald* in 1869. In 1871, he authored his major work, a history of Red River. He became a chief trader in 1878 and retired ten years later. Joseph Hargrave died in Edinburgh in 1894.

Ruth Walker Harvey was the daughter of Corliss and Harriet (née Anderson) Walker, who owned and operated the Walker Theatre in Winnipeg. She was born in Alabama in 1900 and was raised and educated in Winnipeg. She attended the University of Manitoba and served as an editor for the *Manitoban* newspaper. In 1931, Ruth married Howard Harvey, a professor of languages. They had one son, Michael. They lived for many years in Minnesota, where her husband was on the faculty of the University of Rochester. She published her memoirs, titled *Curtain Time*, in 1949. Ruth passed away in Florida in 1996.

Samuel Hearne was born in London, England in 1745. He left school at the age of 11 and joined the Royal Navy. He saw action during the Seven Years War serving under Captain Samuel Hood. In 1763, Hearne left the navy and joined the Hudson's Bay Company in 1766. He led three overland expeditions in search of the Northwest Passage and travelled further north than any other European before him. In 1774, he established Fort Cumberland, the HBC's first inland trading post. He returned to England in 1787 and began writing *A Journey from Prince of Wales's Fort in Hudson's Bay to the Northern Ocean*. It was published in 1795, three years after his death from dropsy at the age of 47.

Martha Hochheim is a first generation Winnipegger born and raised by immigrants of Mennonite heritage. She married Klaus Hochheim, also a first generation Winnipegger, whose parents were German immigrants. Their heritage plays a large part in how they raised their children and the traditions they celebrate.

Margaret Laurence (née Wemyss) is a major figure in Canadian literature, best known for her novels, *The Stone Angel* and *The Diviners*. She was born in 1926 and grew up in Neepawa. She attended United College in Winnipeg (which later became the University of Winnipeg) and received a B.A. in English Literature in 1947. Margaret married Jack Laurence after graduation and they moved to England in 1949. Her husband's job as a hydraulic engineer took them to British Somaliland in 1950 and then to Ghana in 1952, where they lived for five years. They had two children, Jocelyn and David, during this period. They returned to Canada in 1957. Margaret separated from her husband in 1962 and spent a year in England before moving to Lakefield, Ontario. In 1986, she was diagnosed with late-stage lung cancer. To spare herself and her family from further suffering, she ended her life on January 5, 1987.

Story Contributors

Nellie McClung (née Mooney) was a suffragist and writer who played a leading role in gaining the right to vote for women in Manitoba. She was born in Chatsworth, Ontario in 1873 to John and Letitia Mooney. Her family moved to the Souris Valley region of Manitoba in 1880, where she was raised on a homestead. She became a teacher at the age of 16 and taught school until her marriage to Robert Wesley McClung in 1896. In 1914, they moved to Edmonton, Alberta, where they raised five children. She was elected to the Alberta legislature in 1921 and served one term. Nellie McClung was one of the "Famous Five" who petitioned the Supreme Court of Canada to have women included in the definition of "persons" who could serve in the Senate of Canada. In her later years, she focused on her literary career and authored 16 books in total. She passed away in British Columbia in 1951.

Gladys McKay (née Alsaker) was born in La Rivière in 1902 to Samuel and Christina Alsaker. Her father was Norwegian and her mother was from Sweden. They settled in La Rivière in 1893. She had six siblings, but three died in infancy and a sister, Edna, died at age 11. Gladys worked as a teacher until her marriage to Harold McKay in 1930. They had two daughters together.

Sheila McKay grew up in Portage la Prairie, where her parents owned and operated KoKo's Family Restaurant. After graduating from high school, Sheila moved to Winnipeg and trained as a doctor's assistant at Herzing College. She worked at a medical office for several years before deciding to explore other opportunities. After working at a number of jobs, she decided to pursue hairstyling as a career a few years ago and attended MC College, where she received her training. She is currently a hairstylist in Winnipeg.

George Simpson McTavish (ca. 1863–1943) was born in Rupert's Land to George and Mary McTavish. His father, George Simpson McTavish, Sr., was an Inspecting Chief Factor for the Hudson's Bay Company. George Simpson, Jr. began his career with the Hudson's Bay Company in 1879 as an apprentice clerk at York Factory. He left the HBC in 1892 and became a manager of a salmon cannery in British Columbia. He married Lilian Gurd in 1901. They had no children. He died in Victoria at the age of 80.

Jens Munk (1579–1628) was a Dano-Norwegian explorer. His story in this anthology details his third attempt at searching for the Northwest Passage, which ended with the loss of most of his crew. Although Munk had plans to return to the New World, his failing health prevented it. He subsequently served as a sea captain in the royal navy of Christian IV and saw combat in the Thirty Years War. He died in 1628.

Theresa Oswald is a former NDP MLA and provincial minister. She was born and raised in Winnipeg. Before entering politics, she was an educator and school administrator, and was the vice-principal at Victor Mager School. She was first elected in 2003 as the MLA for Seine River and re-elected in 2007. She was the minister responsible for Healthy Child Manitoba from 2004–2006 and then served as Minister of Health. After an unsuccessful leadership bid in 2015, she chose not to seek re-election.

Margaret Dennis Owen is a Winnipeg writer and a retired school teacher. She has been writing since 1972, and has published many articles. Margaret has degrees in Arts and Education from the University of Manitoba, and received her M.A. in English Literature in 2008. She and her husband Bill have three children, Bruce, Nancy and Geoffrey, and seven grandchildren, Stewart, Alexander, Michelle, Laura, Margaret, Madeline and Katherine.

Joseph Payjack, Jr. is the son of Anna (née Derbowka) and Joseph Payjack. He married Denise Lussier in 1952 and they had three children together. Joseph worked for many years in the hospitality and alcoholic beverage industries. His wife passed away in 2013. He resides in Winnipeg.

Petrosha is a Ukrainian-Canadian blogger who likes to share her heritage with her many followers. She presently lives in Vancouver, B.C. but grew up in a small village just outside of Dauphin, Manitoba. She enjoys sharing her Ukrainian traditions and her recollections of growing up in a Ukrainian-Canadian home. Along with these slice-of-life stories in her blog, Petrosha includes many traditional Ukrainian recipes handed down to her by her late mother and other relatives and friends.

Marcel Pitre bought his first computer at the age of 70 to write up the history and family stories for a family reunion in 1999 and he hasn't stopped since then. His writings include numerous pieces for the local newspapers, family and local military histories, and three self-published books—a local history of his home of Pine Falls, Manitoba; a collection of personal essays from his life; and a photo book of the demolition of the Pine Falls paper mill. He has many fond memories of Christmas growing up in a family of nine in the Lac du Bonnet area, where sleigh rides and Mother's pâté were holiday highlights throughout his childhood in the 1930s–1940s.

Brandy Reid is a mom to two very active hockey-obsessed boys. Brandy was born and raised in Cranberry Portage and has now lived in Flin Flon for 15 years. She returned to the outside world of work in 2014 and is currently employed as an administrative assistant for her local health authority. As a former young adult librarian, Brandy loves to read and promote reading every day. Brandy proudly admits that she is a bit addicted to social media, especially Twitter, and was an avid blogger once upon a time.

Story Contributors

Charles Douglas Richardson was originally from Grenfell, Saskatchewan. He was the fifth of seven children in the family of Benjamin and Margaret Richardson. He attended the Manitoba Agricultural College and graduated with a bachelor of science degree in agriculture in 1914. He enlisted in 1915 with the Princess Patricia's Canadian Light Infantry (PPCLI) and went overseas in 1916. Charles was killed in action at Vimy Ridge in 1917. He was 25 years old.

Trish Suzanne was born and raised in Winnipeg and is currently living in Victoria, B.C. Her Finnish grandparents retired to Port Arthur, Ontario in the 1960s, where and when her story takes place.

Alexandre-Antonin Taché was the first Archbishop of St. Boniface. He was the son of Charles Taché and Louise-Henriette de Labroquerie. He attended seminary school at the College du St. Hyacinthe and the Montreal Theological Seminary. After completing his Oblate novitiate in 1845, Taché was sent west to the Red River Settlement with Father Pierre Aubert to establish a mission at St. Boniface. Upon the death of Bishop Provencher in 1854, Taché succeeded him as the Bishop of St. Boniface. In 1869, he was recalled from Rome by the Canadian government to deal with the rebellion in Red River. He returned to Manitoba in 1870 and acted as a liaison between Louis Riel's provisional government and the Canadian government in negotiating the Manitoba Act. Taché became archbishop in 1871, when St. Boniface became a metropolitan diocese. He died at the age of 70 on June 22, 1894 in St. Boniface.

Grace Warkentin was born and raised in Steinbach, where her father owned the Steinbach Bargain Store. She comes from a large family of eleven children (nine girls and two boys). Her parents, Mr. and Mrs. Peter D. Reimer, were prominent members of the local business and church community. Grace married her high school sweetheart, Wilf Warkentin, and they moved to Morden together with their three children, where Wilfred had purchased a Chrysler dealership. In Morden, she owned and operated Grace's Clothes Cupboard, a women's fashion boutique. In the early '70s, she was also a rural correspondent for the *Winnipeg Tribune*. Grace is a published poet and has won awards from the Canadian Authors Association (Winnipeg) and the Writers' Collective. She has also served as director on two national boards, for Tourism Industry of Canada and the Canadian Mental Health Association.

Eileen Wilson (née Chandler) was born in 1915 to William Chandler and Eileen Denison. She was raised in Winnipeg and graduated from Rupert's Land College (which later became Balmoral Hall). She married Clifford Parnell Wilson in 1940. They lived in Winnipeg until 1958, when they moved to Calgary, where they lived for two years. In 1960, they moved to Ottawa and spent seven years there. They then retired to Victoria ("where they didn't have to shovel snow"). Regardless of where she was, Eileen was very active in the community and was a supporter of the arts. She died in Vancouver in 2005.

Recipe Contributors

- Carol Anderson and Katherine Mallinson
- Margaret Fast
- Ashley Gaden
- Claire Herbert
- Mary-Ann Kirkby
- Crystal LeGoff
- Sheila McKay
- Margaret Dennis Owen
- Petrosha
- Stéphane Pichon
- Melanie Reimer
- Trish Suzanne
- Kristine Tubiera
- Mark Vajcner
- Grace Warkentin
- Helen Webber and Marie Woolsey

Acknowledgements

I would like to thank the following individuals and organizations for their assistance at various stages of the project:

- Liv Albert
- Jim Ballowes
- Caitlin Blackmore
- Canadian Broadcasting Corporation
- Flin Flon Heritage Project
- Gordon Goldsborough
- Mary-Ann Kirkby
- Library and Archives Canada
- Manitoba Historical Society
- Andrea Martin
- McNally Robinson Booksellers
- Michele Pacheco
- Penguin Random House
- Provincial Archives of Manitoba
- Ryan Schellenberg
- Sears Canada
- Charmaine Sommerfelt
- Libby Stoker-Lavelle
- Andrea Sutcliffe
- Shelley Sweeney
- Sarah Wood
- Darren Yearsley

I would especially like to thank the staff of the University of Manitoba Archives & Special Collections, where I spent many a lunch hour researching material for this anthology. Their assistance was invaluable.

And last, but not least, I would like to sincerely thank everyone who contributed their stories, photos, and recipes for this anthology. Without their contributions, *Manitoba at Christmas* would not have been possible.

Sources

Stories (in order of appearance)

Jens Munk, "Christmas in Nova Dania." From: Gosch, C. C. A. (ed.) *Danish Arctic Expeditions, Book II: The Expedition of Captain Jens Munk to Hudson's Bay in Search of a North-West Passage in 1619–20*, London: Hakluyt Society, 1897. Translated from: Munk, Jens. *Navigatio Septentrionalis*, Copenhagen: Hegel & Son, 1624.

Samuel Hearne, "Hearne's Third Expedition." From: Hearne, Samuel. *A Journey from Prince of Wales's Fort in Hudson's Bay to the Northern Ocean*, Toronto: The Champlain Society, 1911.

Robert M. Ballantyne, "To Absent Friends." From: Ballantyne, R. M., *Hudson's Bay; or, Everyday Life in the Wilds of North America*, London: Thomas Nelson and Sons, 1879, chapter 8.

Alexandre-Antonin Taché, "Archibishop Taché's First Christmas in Manitoba." *Winnipeg Daily Sun*, December 25, 1882.

Joseph J. Hargrave, "A Red River Christmas." *Winnipeg Daily Sun*, December 25, 1882.

John J. Gunn, "The Festive Season in the Olden Days." From: Gunn, John J. *Echoes of the Red : a Reprint of Some of the Early Writings of the Author Depicting Pioneer Days in the Red River Settlements*, Toronto: Macmillan, 1930, pp. 106–109.

Anonymous, "Christmas Morning on the Red River Settlement." *Nor'Wester*, December 11, 1864, p. 3.

An Old Resident, "How Riel's Prisoners Got Their Christmas Dinners." *Winnipeg Daily Sun*, December 25, 1882, p. 4.

Anonymous, "A Notable Dinner at Fort Garry." *Winnipeg Daily Times*, December 24, 1884, p. 1.

Mary FitzGibbon, "A Christmas Ball." From: FitzGibbon, Mary. *A Trip to Manitoba, or Roughing it on the Line*, London: Richard Bentley and Son, 1880, chapter 6.

George Simpson McTavish, "Christmas at York Factory." From: McTavish, George Simpson. *Behind the Palisades*, Victoria: Colonist Printers, 1963, chapter 26.

Emma Louisa Averill, "Christmas at the Averill Homestead." From: Averill, Emma Louisa. *A Journal from Liverpool to the Far West of Manitoba – 1880*, ca. 1881. Archives of Manitoba, Emma Louisa Averill journal, P267/1.

Nellie McClung, "Spruce Boughs and Apple-Jelly Tarts." From: McClung, Nellie. *Clearing in the West: My Own Story*, Toronto: Thomas Allen, 1935, chapter 20.

Salome Halldorson, "Icelandic Christmas." From: Lundar and District Historical Society. *Wagons to Wings: History of Lundar and Districts 1872–1980*, Lundar: Lundar and District Historical Society, p. 184. Reprinted with permission of the Rural Municipality of Coldwell.

Winnipeg Daily Tribune, "One of the Finest Christmas Displays Ever Seen." *Winnipeg Daily Tribune*, December 22, 1900, p. 7. Reprinted with permission of University of Manitoba Archives & Special Collections.

Gladys McKay, "Santa Claus is a Good Lad." From: *Turning Leaves: A History of La Rivière and District*, La Rivière: La Rivière Historical Book Society, 1979, pp. 107–108. Reprinted with permission of Lois Creith (ed.).

William A. Czumer, "The First Galician Christmas at Bachman School." From: Czumer, William A. *Recollections about the Life of the First Ukrainian Settlers in Canada*, Edmonton: Canadian Institute of Ukrainian Studies, 1981. Reprinted with permission of the Canadian Institute of Ukrainian Studies.

Ruth Walker Harvey, "A World of Wonders." From: Harvey, Ruth Walker. *Curtain Time*, Boston: Houghton Mifflin, 1949. Reprinted with permission of Houghton Mifflin Harcourt.

Verena Garrioch, "Turning Back Memory's Happiest Pages." *Winnipeg Tribune*, December 20, 1957, p. 12. Reprinted with permission of University of Manitoba Archives & Special Collections.

Arthur R. Devlin, "Christmas at Asessippi." From: *Manitoba Pageant*, Winter 1974, Volume 19, Number 2. Reprinted with permission of the Manitoba Historical Society.

Charles Douglas Richardson, "Thinking of Home." From: The Canadian Letters & Images Project, Victoria Island University, www.canadianletters.ca. Reprinted with permission of Dr. Stephen Davies, Vancouver Island University.

Sources

Evelina Adams, "The Spanish Flu Comes to Neepawa." From: *Manitoba History*, No. 14, Autumn 1987. Reprinted with permission of Evelina's nephew, Gerald Brown, and the Manitoba Historical Society.

Mabel E. Finch, "Christmas in a New Canadian School." *Grain Growers' Guide*, December 3, 1920, pp. 66–67. Reprinted with permission of Farm Business Communications.

Winnipeg Evening Tribune, "Santa and His Marvels Come Back to City." *Winnipeg Evening Tribune*, November 17, 1928, p. 1. Reprinted with permission of University of Manitoba Archives & Special Collections.

Winnipeg Evening Tribune, "Little Girl's Wish Brings Santa to Hudson's Bay." *Winnipeg Evening Tribune*, November 23, 1928, p. 4. Reprinted with permission of University of Manitoba Archives & Special Collections.

Vera Fryer, "Next Stop, Pine Falls." From: *Manitoba History*, No. 16, Autumn, 1988. Reprinted with permission of the Manitoba Historical Society.

Rose Fyleman, "Winnipeg at Christmas." *Punch*, January 1, 1930. Reprinted with permission of The Society of Authors.

Wayne Chan, "How 'Winnipeg at Christmas' Came to Pass." © Wayne Chan.

Joseph Payjack, Jr., "Riding the Rods." From: Comstock, Eileen. *Sunny Side Up: Fond Memories of Prairie Life in the 1930s*. Calgary: Fifth House Publishing, 2001. Reprinted with permission of Fifth House Publishing.

Eileen Wilson (as Eileen Chandler), "A Vignette of a Winnipeg Winter." From: *The Eagle: Rupert's Land College Magazine*, volume 5, October 1933, pp. 34–36. Reprinted with permission of Balmoral Hall School.

Margaret Laurence, "Upon a Midnight Clear." From: Laurence, Margaret. *Heart of a Stranger*. Toronto: McClelland and Stewart, 1976, pp. 192–199. Reprinted with permission of Penguin Random House and the estate of Margaret Laurence.

Alice and David Didur, "Ukrainian Christmas on the Homestead." © David Didur. Previously published on Children's Health & Safety Association website (www.safekid.org). Excerpt reprinted with permission of David Didur.

Marcel Pitre, "Happenings From Our Farm." © Marcel Pitre. Previously published in Pitre, Marcel. *Traces of an Era*, 2014. Reprinted with permission.

King George VI, "The King's Speech, Christmas 1939." From: en.wikisource.org/wiki/Christmas_Message,_1939.

Margaret Dennis Owen, "The Home Front." From: Owen, Margaret Dennis. *The Home Front: Hopscotch and Heartache while Daddy was at War*, Winnipeg: Heartland Associates, 2011, chapter 7. Reprinted with permission of Margaret Dennis Owen. Abridged for this anthology by Margaret Dennis Owen.

Evelyn Ballantyne, "Christmas Wish." From: *Windspeaker*, December 1, 1997, volume 15, issue 8, p. 17. Reprinted with permission of *Windspeaker* magazine.

Gordon Billings, "Christmas at Our House." © Gordon Billings. Used by permission.

Mary Louise Chown, "Who Are The Saints?" © Mary Louise Chown. An earlier version was previously published on www.marylouisechown.com. Used by permission.

Wayne Chan, "Going to the Big City: Shopping at Eaton's." © Wayne Chan.

Judy Gerstel, "A Tale of Christmas Past at Eaton's." © 2016 ZoomerMedia Ltd. Previously published on EverythingZoomer.com (www.everythingzoomer.com/bedtime-tale-xmas-past-eatons). Reprinted with permission of Judy Gerstel and ZoomerMedia Ltd.

Grace Warkentin, "Memories of the Last Day Before Christmas." © Grace Warkentin. Previously published in *Mennonite Mirror*, volume 10, issue 4, December, 1980, p. 10. Reprinted with permission of Grace Warkentin.

Winnipeg Tribune, "The Unknown Santa: Silver Dollar Is His Trademark." *Winnipeg Tribune*, December 24, 1958, p. 5. Reprinted with permission of University of Manitoba Archives & Special Collections.

Margaret V. Fast, "The Spirit of Christmas." © Margaret V. Fast. Used by permission.

Petrosha, "Oh Christmas Tree!" © Petrosha. Previously published on Petrosha's Blog: petroshasblog.wordpress.com. Reprinted with permission of Petrosha.

Trish Suzanne, "Finnish Christmas Traditions." © Trish Suzanne. Used by permission.

Donna Gamache, "A Christmas to Remember." © Donna Gamache. Used by permission.

Roger Currie, "Guess Who's Coming to Dinner?" Previously published in *Senior Scope*, volume 12, issue 6, December 10, 2013–January 14, 2014, p. 10. © Roger Currie. Reprinted with permission of Roger Currie.

Theresa Oswald, "My Best Present? My Brother." © Theresa Oswald. Previously published in *Winnipeg Free Press*, December 12, 2015, p. E1. Reprinted with permission of Theresa Oswald.

Sources

Leah Boulet, "A Charlie Brown Tree." © Leah Boulet. Used by permission.

Wayne Chan, "The Christmas Wreath." © Wayne Chan.

Erin Hammond, "North of the Highway." © Erin Hammond. Previously published in *Cottage North* magazine, December, 2003, pp. 7–8. Reprinted with permission of Erin Hammond.

Brandy Reid, "Memories of Christmases Past." © Brandy Reid. Previously published on "My Unwritten Life" blog: myunwrittenlife.com. Reprinted with permission of Brandy Reid.

Martha Hochheim, "Christmas at the Hochheims'." © Martha Hochheim. Used by permission.

Jennifer Collerone, "Crossing the Chief Peguis." © Jennifer Collerone. Used by permission.

Sheila McKay, "On the Doorstep." © Sheila McKay. Used by permission.

Recipes (in order of appearance)

"Eaton's Dark Fruitcake." From: Anderson, Carol and Mollinson, Katherine. *Lunch with Lady Eaton: Inside the Dining Rooms of a Nation*, Toronto: ECW Press, 2004, pp. 190–191. Reprinted with permission of ECW Press.

"CNR Plum Pudding." From: *Drummond Spokesman*, November 24, 1939, p. 3.

"Vinarterta." From: Webber, Helen, and Woolsey, Marie. *Black Currants & Caribou*, Calgary: Blueberries & Polar Bears Publishing, 1999. Also previously published online: webberslodges.com/lodge-recipes/vinarterta. Reprinted with permission of Shari Wright and Webber's Lodges.

"Plumi Moos." Contributed by Margaret V. Fast.

"Ukrainian Christmas Eve Holubtsi (Cabbage Rolls)." Contributed by Petrosha. Previously published on Petrosha's Blog: petroshasblog.wordpress.com. Reprinted with permission of Petrosha.

"Pfeffernüsse." Contributed by Grace Warkentin.

"Slovak Kapustnica and Bobalky." Contributed by Mark Vajcner.

"Broccoli Casserole." Contributed by Crystal LeGoff.

"Grandma's Shortbread." Contributed by Crystal LeGoff.

"Christmas Sweets: Delectable Gifts That the Kitchen May Provide." From: *Grain Growers' Guide*, December 9, 1914, p. 9. Reprinted with permission of Farm Business Communications.

"Nan and Auntie Brenda's Guyanese Fruitcake." Contributed by Claire Herbert.

"Stir-Me-Nots." Contributed by Sheila McKay.

"Filipino-Style Grilled Pork Skewers." Contributed by Kristine Tubiera.

"Alexander Küchen." Contributed by Melanie Reimer.

"Stuffing." Contributed by Ashley Gaden.

"Oatcakes." Contributed by Margaret Dennis Owen.

"Tourtière." Contributed by Stéphane Pichon.

"Finnish Cranberry Pudding." Contributed by Trish Suzanne.

"Slush Punch." Contributed by Ashley Gaden.

"Schuten Krapflen." From: Kirby, Mary-Ann, *Secrets of a Hutterite Kitchen*, Toronto: Penguin, 2014, p. 195. Reprinted with permission of Penguin Random House.

Images

Page vi: Image and poem originally from *The Graphic*, Christmas Number, 1878. Library and Archives Canada, Acc. No. R9266-1556, Peter Winkworth Collection of Canadiana.

Page 4: "The Governor of Red River (Capt. Robert Parker Pelly) Driving his Family on the River in a Horse Cariole, circa 1824." Oil by Cosmo Clark, [1951]. Archives of Manitoba, Hudson's Bay Company Archives, HBCA P-244.

Page 10: From Gosch, C. C. A. (ed.) *Danish Arctic Expeditions, Book II: The Expedition of Captain Jens Munk to Hudson's Bay in Search of a North-West Passage in 1619–20*, London: Hakluyt Society, 1897. Translated from: Munk, Jens. *Navigatio Septentrionalis*, Copenhagen: Hegel & Son, 1624.

Page 15: From Ballantyne, R. M. *Hudson's Bay; or, Everyday Life in the Wilds of North America*, London: Thomas Nelson and Sons, 1879, p. 198.

Page 16: "St. Boniface Cathedral and the Grey Nuns' Convent in 1858." Painting by William Henry Edward Napier. Library and Archives Canada, reproduction reference number C-001065, MIKAN 2836247.

Sources

Page 19: "Monseigneur Alex. A. Taché." From David, L.-O. *Monseigneur Alexandre-Antonin Taché, archevêque de Saint-Boniface*, Montreal: Librairie Saint-Joseph, Cadieux & Derome, 1883.

Page 20: "Returning from Midnight Mass in Manitoba." *Canadian Illustrated News*, December 25, 1880. Reproduced from Library and Archives Canada's website: *Canadian Illustrated News*, 1869–1883.

Page 24: "Manitobah." Painting by William Hind, ca. 1862. William George Richardson Hind collection, Library and Archives Canada, C-013965.

Page 28: "Councillors of the Provisional Government of the Métis Nation." Library and Archives Canada, PA-012854/MIKAN 3194516.

Page 34: "Upper Fort Garry in 1860." From: Seaman, Holly S. *Manitoba Landmarks and Red Letter Days: 1610–1920*. Winnipeg: Holly S. Seaman, 1920, p. 50.

Page 36: *Manitou Mercury*, December 25, 1885, p. 3.

Page 50: Library and Archives Canada, Topley Studio fonds, PA-122949, MIKAN 3304711.

Page 51: Rob McInnes Postcard Collection, Winnipeg Public Library.

Page 52: "Views of La Rivière, Manitoba" by Winnipeg Photo Co., British Library, HS85/10/20398.

Page 58: From: Schooling, William. *The Hudson's Bay Company 1670–1920*, London: Hudson's Bay Company, 1920. Plate opposite p. 103.

Page 70: *Grain Growers' Guide*, December 6, 1916, p. 73. Used by permission of Farm Business Communications.

Page 76: Photo courtesy of Gerald Brown. Used by permission.

Page 78: "Interior of school classroom decorated for Christmas concert, c. 1915." Archives of Manitoba, W. J. Sisler Collection 228, N17233.

Page 82: *Swan Lake Echo*, December 20, 1912, p. 1.

Page 85: *Winnipeg Evening Tribune*, November 16, 1928, p. 32. University of Manitoba Archives & Special Collections, *Winnipeg Tribune* fonds. Used by permission of University of Manitoba Archives & Special Collections.

Page 86: *Winnipeg Evening Tribune*, November 17, 1928, p. 1. University of Manitoba Archives & Special Collections, *Winnipeg Tribune* fonds. Used by permission of University of Manitoba Archives & Special Collections.

Page 92: Rob McInnes Postcard Collection, Winnipeg Public Library.

Page 94: City of Toronto Archives, Fonds 1244, Item 2181.

Page 96: "View of Portage Avenue at night during Christmas season looking west from Portage Avenue & Main Street showing Christmas lights." University of Winnipeg Archives, Western Canada Pictorial Index, Delza Longman Collection (A1309-39158).

Page 102: Photo by Amqui. Distributed under Creative Commons license CC BY-SA 3.0, via Wikimedia Commons.

Page 105: Photo courtesy of Marcel Pitre. Used by permission.

Page 109: Photo courtesy of Andrea Sutcliffe. Used by permission.

Page 110: Photos courtesy of Margaret Dennis Owen. Used by permission.

Page 119: Photos courtesy of Gordon Billings. Used by permission.

Page 120: From: Bramley, H. R. and J. Stainer, *Christmas Carols New and Old, First Series*, 1871. Engraving by Brothers Dalziel. Image via Wikimedia Commons.

Page 124: Archives of Ontario. F 229-308-0-714. T. Eaton's fonds. Used by permission of Sears Canada.

Page 125: University of Winnipeg Archives, Western Canada Pictorial Index, Miscellaneous Collection (A0286-09202).

Page 126: *Eaton's Fall and Winter Catalogue 1925–26*. Toronto and Winnipeg: T. Eaton Co., 1925, p. 394. Used by permission of Sears Canada.

Page 127: *Punkinhead, the Sad Little Bear*. Toronto: T. Eaton Co., 1948. University of Manitoba Archives & Special Collections. Charlie Thorson fonds, MSS 248 (A.06-49), Books and Book Material, Box 5. Used by permission of Sears Canada and University of Manitoba Archives & Special Collections.

Page 128: Archives of Ontario. F 229-308-0-909, AO6662. T. Eaton's fonds. Used by permission of Sears Canada.

Page 130: Photo courtesy of the Red Deer Museum + Art Gallery. Used by permission.

Page 131: Photo courtesy of Grace Warkentin. Used by permission.

Page 133: Photo courtesy of Grace Warkentin. Used by permission.

Sources

Page 134: University of Manitoba Archives & Special Collections, *Winnipeg Tribune* Photo Collection, PC 18, (A.81-12), Box 72, Folder 7243, Item 13. Used by permission of University of Manitoba Archives & Special Collections.

Page 138: Photo courtesy of the Flin Flon Heritage Project. Used by permission.

Page 144: Photo courtesy of Donna Gamache. Used by permission.

Page 146: Photo courtesy of Donna Gamache. Used by permission.

Page 147: Photo courtesy of Roger Currie. Used by permission.

Page 149: University of Manitoba Archives & Special Collections, *Winnipeg Tribune* Photo Collection, A.84-49, PC 18, Box 5, Tribune Negatives 5600–7098. Used by permission of University of Manitoba Archives & Special Collections.

Page 150: Winnipeg Building Index. Used by permission of Mary Lochhead, Head Librarian, University of Manitoba Architecture/Fine Arts Library.

Page 152: Watercolour painting by Leah Boulet. Used by permission.

Page 154: Drawing by Leah Boulet. Used by permission.

Page 164: Photos courtesy of Martha Hochheim. Used by permission.

Page 166: Photo courtesy of *The Reminder (Flin Flon)* and the Flin Flon Heritage Project. Used by permission of *The Reminder*.

Page 168: Photo courtesy of Winnipeg Transit. Used by permission.

Page 170: Photo from www.publicdomainpictures.net.

Page 172: *Winnipeg Evening Tribune*, December 23, 1930, p. 20. University of Manitoba Archives & Special Collections, *Winnipeg Tribune* fonds. Used by permission of Sears Canada and University of Manitoba Archives & Special Collections.

Index

A Christmas Carol, 5
Adams, Evelina, 77, 201
Alexander Küchen, 194
Anderson, Carol, 211
Asessippi, 71
Averill, Emma Louisa, 41, 201

Bachman School, 55
Bakers Narrows, 157, 158
Ballantyne, Evelyn, 115, 201
Ballantyne, Robert M., 13, 201
Beausejour, 55
Billings, Gordon, 117, 202
Bobalky, 183
Boulet, Leah, 153, 202
Brandon, 46, 148, 190

Cake, Pound, 189
Chan, Wayne, 6, 91, 123, 155, 202
Children's Aid Society, 136
Chown, Mary Louise, 121, 202
Churchill, 9
Collerone, Jennifer, 167, 202
Cookies, Pfeffernüsse, 181
Corn Balls, 188
Currie, Roger, 147, 202
Czumer, William, 55, 203

Dauphin, 141
Devlin, Arthur R., 203
Dickens, Charles, 5
Didur, Alice, 103, 203
Didur, David, 103, 203
Doll, Barbara Ann Scott, 129, 130

Doll, Eaton's Beauty, 126
Duchov, Morris, 135

Eaton's displays, 123
Eaton's Santa Claus Parade, 124
Eaton's Toyland, 129
Eaton's Winnipeg store, 123, 129
Egg River, 11

Fast, Margaret, 139, 178, 203, 211
Finch, Mabel, 79
Finch, Mabel E., 204
FitzGibbon, Mary, 35, 204
Flin Flon, 159, 161
Fraserwood, 79
Fruitcake, Eaton's Dark, 173
Fruitcake, Guyanese, 190
Fryer, Vera, 89, 204
Fudge, Fruit, 189
Fudge, Peanut, 189
Fyleman, Rose, 6, 90, 91, 204

Gaden, Ashley, 195, 199, 211
Gamache, Donna Firby, 145, 204
Garrioch, Verena, 67, 205
George VI, King, 107, 205
Gerstel, Judy, 129, 205
Good Deed Club, 132
Gunn, John J., 25, 205

Halldorson, Salome, 47, 205
Hammond, Erin, 157, 205
Hargrave, Joseph J., 205
Harvey, Ruth Walker, 59, 206

Hearne, Samuel, 11, 206
Herbert, Claire, 190, 211
Hochheim, Martha, 165, 206

Kapustnica, 183
Kirkby, Mary-Ann, 211
Kiwanis Club, 113
Knowles Centre, 136
Kobold & Co., 49

La Rivière, 53
Lac du Bonnet, 105
Laurence, Margaret, 97, 206
Le Croissant bakery, 197
LeGoff, Crystal, 211
Letters to Santa, 123

Macdonald, Jean, 91
MacGregor, 117
MacLeod, Terry, 91
Mallinson, Katherine, 211
Marlborough Hotel, 113
McClung, Nellie, 45, 207
McKay, Gladys, 207
McKay, Sheila, 169, 207, 211
McLennan, Sadie, 71
McTavish, George Simpson, Jr., 37, 207
Minnedosa, 44, 145, 204
Munk, Jens, 9, 207

Neepawa, 77, 97
Northwest Passage, 11
Norway House, 22
Nougat, French, 188
Nova Dania, 9

Oatcakes, 196
Oswald, Theresa, 151, 208
Owen, Margaret Dennis, 111, 196, 208, 211

Payjack, Joseph, Jr., 93, 208
Petrosha, 141, 179, 208, 211
Pichon, Stéphane, 197, 211
Pilot Mound, 49
Pine Falls, 89
Pitre, Marcel, 105, 153, 208
Plumi Moos, 178
Port Arthur, Ontario, 143

Portage la Prairie, 67, 200, 202, 205, 207
Punkinhead, 126

Red River Settlement, 21, 25, 27
Reid, Brandy, 161, 208
Reimer, Melanie, 194, 211
Richardson, Charles, 209
Riel, Louis, 29
Royal Alexandra Hotel, 93, 113
Ruthenian Training School, 55

Schuten Krapflen, 200
Shellmouth, 72
Shoal Lake, 49
Shriners' Hospital, 136
Slush Punch, 199
Spanish Flu, 77
St. Agnes School, 136
Ste. Anne, 49
Steinbach, 131
Stonewall, 82
Suzanne, Trish, 143, 198, 209, 211

Taché, Alexandre-Antonin, 17
Tourtière, 197
Tubiera, Kristine, 193, 211

Upper Fort Garry, 29, 31

Vajcner, Mark, 183, 211
Vinarterta, 176
Virden, 82
Vista, 77

Walker Theatre, 59
Warkentin, Grace, 131, 181, 211
Wawanesa, 45
Webber's Lodges, 176
Webber, Helen, 176, 211
Wilson, Eileen, 209
Winnipeg, 17, 35, 59, 93, 95, 111, 129, 135, 147, 149, 151, 155, 165, 167
Winnipeg at Christmas (poem), 6, 90
Winnipeg Boys' Club, 136
Winnipeg Grenadiers, 111
Woolsey, Marie, 176, 211

York Factory, 13, 37